JEFFREY M. SAUVE

MURDER AT
MINNESOTA
POINT

MURDER AT MINNESOTA POINT

Unraveling the Captivating Mystery of a Long-Forgotten True Crime

JEFFREY M. SAUVE

North Star
—EDITIONS—

Mendota Heights, Minnesota

To Lena,
you are not forgotten

First Edition
Second Printing, 2022

Book and cover design by Sarah Taplin
Book layout by Claire Vanden Branden
Cover image © Shutterstock

ISBN
978-0-578-34139-2 (paperback)
978-0-578-34140-8 (ebook)

Distributed by North Star Editions, Inc.
2297 Waters Drive
Mendota Heights, MN 55120
www.northstareditions.com

Printed in the United States of America

Table of Contents

PREFACE

A close friend asked, "What are the nightmares trying to tell you?" I had wrestled to answer that question for nearly six years. The journey down the dark rabbit hole started in November 2012.

In my work as an archivist for both St. Olaf College and the Norwegian-American Historical Association in Northfield, Minnesota, I was often asked to research past events or individuals. A useful tool at my disposal was digitized historic newspapers.

In one such foray into the printed past, a curious, unrelated headline caught my attention: "Is All a Mystery" (*Duluth News Tribune*, August 23, 1894). The article's tantalizing introduction hooked me: "There is nothing but mystery surrounding the body of the woman found at O-at-ka beach yesterday afternoon. The chief of police and the city detectives said last night that they were unable to find any clue that would tend to unravel the mystery. There is no doubt in the mind of the authorities that the woman, whoever she may be, was murdered."

Over the course of the next two years, I spent countless hours amassing hundreds of clippings regarding the mysterious crime, which would eventually form the basis for the nonfiction *Murder at Minnesota Point: Unraveling the Captivating Mystery of a*

Long-Forgotten True Crime. As a writer, my process is to initially frame the story in my head, typically before falling asleep. After my first nightmare occurred, I simply shrugged it off. But as I continued to develop the manuscript, the disturbing dreams revisited me regularly, whether or not I had contemplated the sordid tale at bedtime.

Each nightmare held a similar murky, dark scene of a desolate shoreline, foreboding violence. A slender arm emerged from the cool shallows of Lake Superior, reaching out to grasp my neck. Fleeing, sinister eyes hidden within the dunes followed me while seagulls screeched overhead. My hands were oddly bloodied, my heart pounding. At this point I always awoke, sometimes in a sweat, breathing quickly, startling my wife, Evelyn.

Recurring dreams are not unique to me. Following the unexpected death in 1979 of my older seventeen-year-old brother, Steve, I experienced essentially the same dream off and on for more than a decade: At a bus stop, a still slim, but older man disembarks from a Greyhound bus. We greet each other as long-lost brothers, and I ask Steve, "Where have you been these many years?" A short, simple dream, but bearing a foundation for deeper exploration.

After Steve's passing, my family did not seek counseling nor discuss openly what had transpired. A mystery shrouded the event, and like a fog, it hung low over our family, dissipating slightly by decades of avoidance of resurrecting painful memories. For me, the dreams stopped after I visited his graveside with my mother. Her voice trembled as she recalled how my brother barely survived birth and his creativity and sensitivity as a child; his sweetness and love are forever etched in her heart.

The moment was transformative, and after saying the Lord's Prayer in unison, I felt an inner peace as we left.

The same peace could not be said for me as I delved into the century-old Duluth crime. Family and friends worried that my compulsion had developed into an unhealthy habit to tell the story. Several urged me to leave it alone for my own good. The balancing act of a narrative that honored the slain woman paled to the honest assessments by those who cared for me.

Before relinquishing the project completely, I turned to my swimming buddy Qiguang Zhao, affectionately known as Professor Q. As a Chinese scholar at neighboring Carleton College in Northfield, he and I both enjoyed meeting at the local senior center for lap swimming followed by a relaxing conversation in the hot tub. Qiguang, ever friendly and helpful, posed mindful questions and suggested different approaches that might help alleviate my occasional nightly sufferings.

In early March 2015, he pointedly asked, "So what would you tell or ask her [the murdered woman] if given a chance?" I did not have a ready response, and he said, "Well, let's talk in a few weeks. I'm off tomorrow for spring break." On March 12, the man who was widely known for his interest in Marco Polo was overcome by a riptide and drowned off the coast of Miami. For the next three years, I stepped completely away from *Murder at Minnesota Point*. As the story faded from my everyday life, so did the frightful dreams.

In late summer 2018, my family and I stood on the observation deck of the eighty-foot high Enger Tower located in the hills of Duluth, overlooking Minnesota Point and O-at-ka Beach, the site of the heinous act that occurred in 1894. A middle-aged couple who stood nearby struck up a conversation with me, and before long, they gleaned that I was a writer and historian. The fellow asked me what I was currently working on. For something relatable, I pointed out the beach in the foreground and proceeded to give a short talk regarding the events that captured the nation's attention in the late nineteenth century.

I elaborated on the context of the times. Millions of immigrants sought the promise of America during the Gilded Age, a time marked by great prosperity and the rapid expansion of technology and industry. The era also witnessed a variety of sensationalized killers leading up to the individual whom I had been researching. There was the August 1892 Lizzie Borden case that still fascinates true-crime enthusiasts. At age six, I recall my introduction to evil by skipping rope on the school playground with classmates who recited the rhyme: "Lizzie Borden took an axe/And gave her mother forty whacks/When she saw what she had done/She turned and gave her father forty-one."

The following summer in 1893, Chicago hosted the World's Columbian Exposition, a monumental fair that attracted tens of thousands of tourists. Preying on numerous women visitors was psychopathic serial killer H.H. Holmes. His exploits were detailed in Erik Larson's masterfully told book, *The Devil in the White City: Murder, Magic, and Madness at the Fair That Changed America* (2003).

Before I finished my impromptu Enger Tower talk, an additional seven or eight people had gathered to hear me out. They were gobsmacked! A few asked if I could repeat what they had missed earlier. Walking down the 105 steps, I could not help but notice a wary eye from Evelyn. No doubt I was excited by the positive reception of my story, but dare I revisit it once again? During our drive home to Northfield, I told her what Qiguang had asked me in 2015. Without hesitating, she encouraged me to visit the murdered woman's grave and speak to her in person.

Easier said than done, I thought. Through my extensive research I understood the victim was reinterred in Minneapolis, but not a single clipping provided the cemetery name. Evelyn commented that databases are updated and new materials are posted all the time. Perhaps I should check again? She was correct. Before long, I learned the woman's remains had been placed in the historic Lakewood Cemetery.

On a beautiful fall day, October 21, 2018, Evelyn and I traveled to the cemetery and spent ninety minutes searching for the gravesite, Section PG11, Row 112, Grave 8. Nearing frustration, a security guard stopped by in a vehicle, asking us if we needed help. He had noticed our zigzagging about. "Did you know there's an app to find the grave?" he asked. Within minutes, Evelyn's cell phone directed us to the grave's location.

Sensing my need for privacy, Evelyn continued on to admire the many interesting headstones nearby. There is something awkward and yet beautiful at the same time when talking to the dead. Here, under recently scattered crimson autumn leaves, lay a forgotten soul—a footnote in a lurid tale. But, of course, she was much more than that—she was a person of worth, no matter her station, education, gender, or heritage. She was a human to the core with a desire to love and be loved.

Soon after the visit, a calmness and understanding propelled me to return to the manuscript unhindered and complete what I had set out to do many years before. The following narrative is faithful to its unfolding, and quotations are verbatim as printed in various period newspapers. Discrepancies between sources are explained in chapter endnotes. She is remembered.

Jeffrey M. Sauve
Northfield, Minnesota
December 2021

Nowadays it is only in summer that a little life, other than that of its few inhabitants, shows itself on Minnesota Point—when camping-parties and picnic-parties go down by three miles of shaky tramway to Oatka Beach. During all the rest of the year that sandy barren, with its forlorn decaying houses and its dreary growth of pines stunted by the harsh lake winds, is forgotten and desolate.

Now and then is heard the cry of a gull flying across it slowly; and always against its outer side—with a thunderous crash in times of storm, in times of calm with a sad soft lap-lapping—surge or ripple the deathly cold waters of Lake Superior: waters so cold that whoever drowns in them sinks quickly—not to rise again (as the drowned do usually), but for all time, in chill companionship with the countless dead gathered there through the ages, to be lost and hidden in those icy depths.

—Thomas A. Janvier, "A Duluth Tragedy,"
Harper's New Monthly Magazine, August 1899

CHAPTER ONE
A Body Found

Wednesday, August 22, 1894

Guy Browning, seven, stood on Duluth's O-at-ka Beach, his heart pounding. Ahead of him on the deserted, sandy ribbon of shoreline, driftwood lay heaped like a pile of bleached bones. A motionless hand protruded from the watery debris, reaching out in vain. Around the slight wrist a silver bracelet glinted in the midmorning sun.

Slowly, he turned his head in the direction of the dunes, wary of meeting unwanted, evil eyes. A seagull's screech startled Browning, sending him racing more than a half mile to home. His bare feet dug hard into the wet sand, leaving small footprints soon lost forever. As he neared his house, gasping for breath, the boy yelled for his mother, Mary, who immediately reported the matter to the police. From that moment on, the mystery of the dead woman's grim demise captured the nation's attention.[1]

Minnesota Point streetcar, Duluth, Minnesota, ca. 1890s. Courtesy of the Duluth Public Library, Duluth, Minnesota.

By early afternoon, Duluth Police Chief Harry Armstrong, Captain Sam Thompson, St. Louis County Coroner Dr. John Eklund, and detectives Bob Benson and Tom Hayden boarded the tug *Pathfinder,* embarking to O-at-ka Beach on the harbor side of Minnesota Point. As the boat plied the cold, blue waters under overcast skies, the crescent-shaped peninsula lay before them. Covered in a forest of scrub pine and thickets of birch, the seven-mile spit, with an average width of eight-hundred feet, is the largest freshwater sandbar in the world.

For centuries, until the 1854 Treaty of La Pointe, the Ojibwe regularly camped on the Point over the summer months, naming the site Neiashi or Shagawamik, meaning "a point of land." In August 1780, the great battle of Black Beaver of the

Ojibwa versus Black Eagle of the Dakota took place on the lands between the St. Louis and Nemadji Rivers. According to tribal historian Christine Carlson, the battle ended at O-at-ka Beach with approximately one hundred dead.

Following the treaty, the land opened for settlement by predominantly Europeans pioneers. Within two decades, in 1871, a canal was dug at the base of the Point, which allowed direct shipping access from Lake Superior to the calm waters and harbor of St. Louis Bay. By 1894, the sparsely populated village known as Park Point had developed, including a plodding horse-drawn streetcar that carried passengers over three miles from the canal to O-at-ka Beach.

To accommodate the numerous campers, day picnickers, and boaters, a bathhouse that rented bathing suits was unveiled

Duluth, Minnesota, 1892. The seven-mile sand spit known as Minnesota Point in background. Courtesy of the University of Minnesota Duluth, Kathryn A. Martin Library, Northeast Minnesota Historical Collections.

in July. Undercover officers in plain clothes were assigned to look "after the promiscuous bathers who throng to the shore and fail to wear bathing trunks or suits."

And notices in the press read: "An attendant will be in charge who will supply bathing suits and every effort will be made to make the place popular with all classes."

These classes included tradesmen, household servants, artisans, professionals, old-money families, and fashionable nouveau riche. It is worth noting that beachgoers were also diverse. One blurb from August 2, 1893, is racially insensitive but provides an early record: "A complaint was made this morning against Frank Pickett, the fellow charged with selling quarrel-provoking beer to the colored people who held a picnic down on O-at-ka Beach yesterday."

For Duluthians, the beautiful, four-block-long beach between 39th and 43rd streets had only recently come into its own as the only true resort in the vicinity. Much of O-at-ka's early success was due in part to the efforts of Captain Byron B. Inman, known affectionately as "Commodore Inman," a prominent tug owner.

Recognizing Duluth's emerging popularity as a tourist destination in the spring of 1889, Inman purchased the propeller steamer *John C. Liken*. "The idea struck him," recounted the *Duluth Evening Herald* in August 1900, that "it would be a pretty good scheme to fix up a place to land passengers and run excursions."

With a pier in place, daily round-trip excursions started on July 4, 1889, at twenty-five cents per adult, ten cents per child. Highlighting the holiday weekend included De Feleese's celebrated Italian string band, which furnished music on the boat and in the grove, and fun and games with tub races and a greased pig. For the remainder of the summer, the *Liken* left the Lake Avenue dock every couple of hours on Wednesdays, Fridays, and Sundays providing passengers a joyful day at the beach. "Go for a day in the sand, or take tea on the beach," and "No improper characters allowed on the grounds," read the newspaper enticements. Inman's venture proved a great success, netting him a handsome sum of $500 on the first day alone.

As a matter of note, the naming of O-at-ka Beach was also credited to Inman. The *Duluth Evening Herald* further stated: "It is generally supposed that the name is an old Indian appellation.

It is probably an Indian name, but it is not of local origin. ...
On a card tacked up in the engine room of the tug [*Liken*],
Capt. Inman found the name 'Oa-at-ka.' It sounded good and
he immediately applied it to the new resort. It stuck, and it has
stayed there ever since, though during the past year the spelling
has been changed so that the 'a' in the first syllable is omitted.
There is an Oa-at-ka Beach near Bay City, Michigan, which is
probably the original."[2]

When the tug *Pathfinder* docked at O-at-ka Beach, the authorities were met by a nervous young Browning and his mother.
After introductions, the boy was questioned about what had
transpired that morning. His mother had sent him to collect
driftwood for the stove, as yet another chilly and rainy day was
forecast. Around ten thirty a.m., he left home. About a half
mile beyond the bathhouse, he came upon the woman's body.

Browning agreed to show authorities where he found her,
and immediately the party started along the isolated shoreline.
Mary Browning held her son's left hand as they walked along.
She knew he was frightened at confronting the horrible sight
once again. Soon the boy stopped and simply pointed ahead,
not uttering a word. Then he pulled his mother to turn around
and the two headed home.

At the scene, the police figured the body, partially buried
under driftwood, rested about three and a half miles east of
the canal. First, Thompson, a former city coroner, proceeded
to remove the debris that encased the poor soul. To the men's
disbelief, her head was tightly wrapped in a brown cape lined
with wine-colored satin. Reportedly, when unwrapped, blood

Tugboat Pathfinder *and crew, Duluth, Minnesota, ca. 1900. Courtesy of the University of Minnesota Duluth, Kathryn A. Martin Library, Northeast Minnesota Historical Collections.*

spurted from the nose and a deep gash on the backside of her head. Her lovely brown hair was matted in blood.

Eklund observed teeth marks on her small hands. Bruises around her neck attested to a violent struggle and the possibility of having been choked into unconsciousness, whereupon her skull was fractured by several blows with a blunt instrument. Near her lay the presumed murder weapon: a rough, heavy, oak stick about four feet long, stained with blood. At one end of the club was a sharp point like a tent stake. A switch of false brown hair and a piece of a tortoiseshell comb were also discovered close by.

Her brown serge skirt and matching waist jacket suggested a person of good station. The undergarments were new and made of quality material, including a silk wrapper. She wore rather new-looking shoes, high-laced with leather tips. One was slightly torn on the side, but neither had scuff marks. Based upon the most probable scenario, Armstrong conjectured the woman was newly married and the clothing had been purchased in contemplation of a wedding trip.

On her left hand she wore two rings. A plain, eighteen-carat, large, gold band sat on her middle finger with a wart just below it. Her third finger featured a small, silver ring with an oval-shaped top—speculated as a wedding ring. On her right wrist she wore a charm bracelet, which had been first noticed by Browning. Twelve dime-sized bangles dangled with six of them engraved: "Father," "Mother," "Sister," "Brother," "Mabel," and "May." At her throat was pinned a gold enamel Egyptian-inspired brooch. Imitation rhinestone earrings accessorized her dress. None of the articles of clothing carried any mark of ownership. Her pockets contained neither money nor paper, which might shed light on her identity.

Her skin was light complexioned with a mole under her chin. She measured approximately five foot six and weighed about 130 pounds. Because her face did not show discoloration, authorities believed she had been alive within the past twenty-four hours. Members of the party agreed the actions of the water could not have deposited the thirtyish-year-old woman in such a manner. She had been placed there by design, not drowned, within the last twelve hours; only her lifeless blue eyes held the identity of her brutal assailant.

At five o'clock the body was ferried by tug to Bayha's morgue, located on First Avenue West. Undertakers at the time commonly doubled as furniture purveyors because of their skill in cabinet and coffin-making. Bayha & Co. advertised, "A flash of lightning may frighten you, but our prices on furniture will surprise you." Yet another sideline business of Bayha's was their City Carpet Cleaning Works.

Detectives from the neighboring port cities of Superior, Wisconsin, and Duluth convened to examine the remains more closely. After conferring, they agreed she was completely unknown to them. An initial plan was set forth: unless identified in the near future, she would be photographed and buried. A baffling mystery was at hand.

Although Duluth had only been established twenty-five years earlier, it had recently become a bustling metropolis likened to the next San Francisco. What was once a small town of 4,000 in 1880 now boasted a flourishing population nearing 40,000 energetic and prosperous people, bolstering one of the world's greatest freshwater inland ports. Grain, iron ore, and lumber were exported through the harbor.

Progress was evident with the terminus of six railroads, twenty-four miles of electric street railways, electric and gas lighting, elegant hotels, and pleasant homes. Neighborhood streets were carved out of the solid rock that formed the hills. Wide sidewalks extended throughout the city, often bordered by tended lawns and leafy trees. The business blocks downtown featured stately edifices six to ten stories in height.

Without a doubt, Duluth's vibrancy could not shield itself from a seamy underbelly where sinister crime lurked in the

THE RECORD OF CRIME

Cases Where Human Life Has Been Taken
in St. Louis County During Two
Decades Past.

Eighty-Six Assaults of High Degree Found
On the Court Records of Twenty-
Four Years.

Coroners' Juries Have Also Sat On Sixty-
Nine Lifeless Bodies Killed By Parties Unknown.

The assassin's revolver, knife and
bludgeon have played an important

*A tantalizing 1893 newspaper clipping detailing past crimes committed in
Duluth, Minnesota. Courtesy of the Minnesota Historical Society Newspaper
Digital Hub.*

ZENITH CITY'S DARK SIDE

Duluth's first recorded murder took place in 1869: the stabbing of George Northrup. Over the course of the next twenty-five years, violent crimes were committed in nearly every corner of the city.

In 1875, a well-publicized case involved fifteen-year-old Hattie Russell and her seducer, liquor dealer John Pugsley. On the evening of March 5, 1875, Russell admittedly mortally wounded Pugsley by shooting him in the back. He had repeatedly denied that he was the father of her one-year-old child. Although considered wayward, she evoked the sympathies of the ladies of Duluth who felt sorry for her story of wrongs committed against her and sought an attorney on her behalf. Russell was acquitted on the ground of insanity.

In 1885, a knife-wielding Maurice Mayer tried to "cut a suit of clothes out of Bruce Emil Dietz's anatomy." John B. Hynes in 1892 chopped his wife, May, with a hatchet and pounded her with a hammer; miraculously, she survived. He received a slap on the wrist for attempted murder and was sentenced to two years and seven months in Stillwater State Prison.

The last murder to take place in Duluth before the woman was discovered on O-at-ka Beach occurred a year before on July 5, 1893. Leslie Pikkarinen shot Henry Clyne in a West Duluth restaurant out of spite for being addressed as "Pinkerton," alluding to the famous detective agency. Surprisingly, Pikkarinen did not mind acquaintances calling him "Whitey," an appellation suggested by his personal appearance resembling an albino. He was sentenced to an indefinite "reformatory plan" in Stillwater.

Sources: "A Well Known Merchant Shot by a Woman," *St. Cloud Journal*, March 11, 1875, 2. "The Murder of John Pugsley," *The Grange Advance*, March 16, 1875, 7; and "Minnesota Newslets," *Stillwater Messenger*, June 11, 1875, 4; "The Record of Crime," *Duluth Evening Herald*, March 11, 1893, 1; and "Criminal Cases On," *Duluth Evening Herald*, September 25, 1893, 6.

shadows. It was described as a wide-open city "where liquor, loose women, and confidence men could be found in abundance." Much of this was due to the mining and lumber camps in the region. Men from these camps were described as rough in character and stunted in morals, and when under the influence, feared neither consequences nor authority. In 1892, there were at least fifty places in the city without a municipal license where liquor was sold at any hour day or night. Down by the wharves, more than thirty houses of prostitution existed.

Superior Street looking east from Seventh Avenue West, Duluth, Minnesota, ca. 1895. Courtesy of the University of Minnesota Duluth, Kathryn A. Martin Library, Northeast Minnesota Historical Collections.

The crime of murder occurred rather frequently, tallying seventy souls since 1869, the latest having taken place the year before in July 1893. The *Duluth Evening Herald* quipped, "The assassin's revolver, knife and bludgeon have played an important part in keeping down the 'surplus' of human life in this neck of the woods."

News of the supposed murder of the woman discovered the day before on O-at-ka Beach not only captured the attention and conversation of many but also troubled those who worried if the killer yet remained in the vicinity. Could he take more victims? In the history of St. Louis County dating to the Minnesota Territorial days of 1856, the coroner's office had dealt with less than a handful of deadly assaults against women. This case, the first unknown female homicide within the city limits, transfixed the locals with a certain morbid curiosity.

From early Thursday morning, August 23, until late at night, hundreds of people stopped by Bayha's morgue to view the embalmed body in hopes of identifying her or at least providing additional clues. In the undertaker's windowless room, lighted only by kerosene lamps, the woman's rigid corpse lay stark and cold on a marble slab. Gasps of shock and spirited whispering accompanied the shuffling of endless feet. To keep the room chilled, large blocks of ice, harvested earlier in the year from Lake Superior, lined the walls. Sawdust layered the blocks to slow their melting, giving the confining space a dank aroma mingled with the smells of death and the subtle sweetness of pine. On a table nearby lay her personal effects, including the bracelet.

Two morgue visitors included Kate Branthurst, a sales lady at Freimuth's dry goods store, and a Miss Anderson. The two of them believed the dead woman was the same person who was alive and well on the streetcar the Tuesday evening before. They were especially certain on account of the distinctive bracelet. Branthurst provided an interview to the *Duluth*

Evening Herald describing their short acquaintance with the victim and her gentleman.

On Tuesday evening they had crossed the canal aboard the free city ferry and then caught a streetcar at Minnesota Point bound for O-at-ka Beach. Before reaching the end of the line, they exited for one of the many summer camps on the Point.

What started as a commune with nature for health and enjoyment by a few campers soon blossomed into a city of tents with over sixty campsites housing an estimated 2,000 campers. During the summer of 1894, Damfino, Hot Water Camp, Koo-Koo Camp, Uncle Tom's Cabin, and others dotted both sides of the peninsula. To most campers nestled in the thick growth of shady pine trees with hammocks strung, the roar and crash of the waves and the nightly bonfires offered a respite from city life, albeit mosquitoes, grasshoppers, and flies were unwelcomed companions.

Branthurst recalled that at seven fifteen p.m., when she and her friend entered the streetcar, six people were already seated, including Mr. J.E. Sisk, a shoe clerk at Burrows; a Mr. Hendrickson who clerked at Weber's store; Mike Daugherty and a Mr. Edwards; and the woman in question and the man at her side. "I remember the woman perfectly," Branthurst said. In her opinion, the woman on the streetcar matched the one in the morgue, adding that she recalled the woman wore a stylish black hat with black trimmings adorned with two large roses in front. The man, in her estimation, was possibly forty or forty-five years old, about five foot eleven, dark complexioned with black curly hair, dark eyes, and a mustache. He wore a dark suit and derby hat.

Also interviewed by the newspaper was fellow streetcar passenger Sisk, who had stopped by Bayha's. He recalled sitting

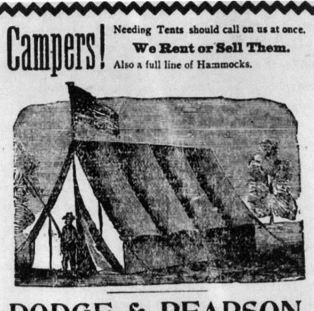

Campers! Needing Tents should call on us at once.
We Rent or Sell Them.
Also a full line of Hammocks.

DODGE & PEARSON,
423 West Superior St., Lyceum Building.

During the summer of 1894, Damfino, Hot Water Camp, Koo-Koo Camp, Uncle Tom's Cabin, and other campsites dotted both sides of Minnesota Point, Duluth, Minnesota. Courtesy of the Minnesota Historical Society Newspaper Digital Hub.

in the corner of the car when the woman and her companion entered and sat down next to him. "I remember the woman's dress, face, and especially the bracelet and bangles." To him she appeared pleasant, smiling, and happy.

Sisk's description of the male companion closely matched Branthurst's: "The man was thirty-five or forty years old, had a dark complexion, eyes, hair, and a dark brown mustache. He wore a black clay worsted suit with a cutaway coat. He had a white shirt and I think a black bow necktie. He probably weighed 160 pounds, was five foot ten or eleven inches tall. I do not remember the style of the collar. I usually notice a man's shoes above all else, but I failed to notice his. I also remember nothing of any jewelry he had on. … Anyway, the man was a pretty slick-looking fellow and had the appearance of one used to wearing good clothes."

The shoe salesman believed they were strangers to Zenith City, a nickname for Duluth purportedly coined many years earlier by Thomas Foster. Sisk overheard the couple make a few observations on the sights, weather, boats, and campers. At some point, the woman suggested to her companion that they should move over to the other side of the car because of the cool lake air. "No," said the man, "I'll put up this window," which he did, Sisk said.

The impression Sisk had of the dark-complexioned man was mixed. "He seemed all right, yet was not so very pleasant, as his tones were a little cranky when speaking about the window." Branthurst's take was nearly the same as Sisk's, mentioning the man was engaged in a newspaper and seemed irritated when the woman spoke to him. Neither of them saw the woman nor her companion again, as they got off at earlier stops on the line—Branthurst and Anderson at Camp Ming-ma-tab and Sisk at Kamp Komfort.

CHAPTER TWO

The Baffling Mystery

~~~~~~~~

At two p.m. Thursday, the slain woman's body was dressed and photographed. The victim's clothing had been washed earlier in the morning by John Armstead, proprietor of Acme Laundry. The undergarments were stained by lake water and bleeding of dye from the brown dress. Undaunted, Armstead and his wife boiled the linens a couple of times. She said, "Those are the garments of a good woman." Her husband concurred: "We do all kinds of washing and these are not such as sporting women [prostitutes] wear."

To the Armsteads, the clothing looked like a wedding outfit: "Everything was new with not a laundry mark to be found. The linen was good quality and made entirely by hand, there not being a machine stitch on it. The underskirt was handsomely, lavishly, and heavily trimmed with expensive work and material. The garters were such as [to] suspend from the waist and they were new."

Carl Thiel, a former actor turned photographer, took several negatives of the body. They were later widely distributed to regional newspapers. The woman's eyes were opened and

AN UNKNOWN VICTIM.

"An Unknown Victim," Duluth, Minnesota, August 1894. Courtesy of the University of Minnesota Duluth, Kathryn A. Martin Library, Northeast Minnesota Historical Collections.

her hair combed back to provide a natural look, considering her ghastly appearance.

The change in looks concerned at least one man who was quoted in the September 1, 1894, *Duluth Evening Herald*. F.B. Spellman said of her altered appearance: "I was talking recently with a lady who saw this dead woman right after she was found on Minnesota Point. ... and the information was given [to] me that the murdered woman had her hair banged down onto her forehead. When she was laid out for inspection her hair was combed back and the photographs taken show that. Now this lady tells me that she saw the dead woman after the hair was combed back and that it made a most marked change in her appearance. That fact may be a stumbling block in the way of her identification."

The following morning, Friday, August 24, detectives Benson and Hayden returned to O-at-ka Beach searching for any overlooked evidence. Sifting through the sand, Benson located another piece of the hair comb. "It was smashed, as if crushed in a hand." He then waded into the shallows and poked about for additional clues to no avail. "There is nothing more to be learned from that quarter," Benson concluded.

He offered a motive for the homicide: "Everything points to the fact that the woman had some money. This induced some scoundrel to marry her, which he did. When he gained complete control of her money, he deliberately took her out to an isolated place and put her out of the way."

The *Duluth Evening Herald* speculated: "There is a possibility, of course, that both the man and woman were murdered. He was a well-to-do-looking fellow and some desperate character may have killed them for their money, and all know that desperate characters do not shun Minnesota Point." The newspaper elaborated that "the man may have been more effectually [*sic*] disposed of just for the purpose of throwing suspicion on him and to blind the authorities and the public. Then, too, there may not have been time to more effectually [*sic*] conceal the body of the woman."

The statement "all know that desperate characters do not shun Minnesota Point" is illustrated by the peninsula's colorful history preceding the August 1894 O-at-ka Beach murder. In February 1886, a gang of so-called thieves dubbed the "Park Point Pirates," dug a cave in the dunes and raided local

Oatka Dance Hall Pavilion and Owl's Roost, Minnesota Point, Duluth, Minnesota, ca. 1892. The pavilion was known for the "desperate characters" who frequented the dance hall. Courtesy of the Duluth Public Library, Duluth, Minnesota.

establishments by night. During their last foray, the thieves stole lumber from R.A. Gray's mill, presumably to build a hideaway. It was reported that Gray located their lair and captured the gang after a "fierce battle," sending the pirates to the penitentiary.

And in mid-August 1892, two bootleggers were caught operating a "blind pig" near O-at-ka Beach. The *Duluth News Tribune* noted, "There is a dancing pavilion at the beach frequented by anything but a genteel crowd, and it is alleged liquor could be purchased within a stone's throw of the place."

Before noon Friday, Chief Armstrong requested dentist Ned McNulty examine the dead woman's teeth. McNulty found several of them were filled with gold, while six were artificial and fastened to an upper plate; four on the left side and two on the right side. To him, the work was "first class" and recently done. Later in the afternoon, he returned to the morgue and made a complete chart of her mouth. The police hoped by sharing it with dentists all over the country, her identity would soon be learned.

As the weekend unfolded, helpful tipsters offered nearly a dozen possible identities to the police. Almost all had little credence, but the two intrepid Duluth detectives nevertheless listened and investigated several leads of missing women, including three separate quarreling couples who split, and suddenly the wife in each case dropped out of sight; a former house servant in Winona; "an inmate [prostitute] at a disorderly house" in West Superior; a former employee of a local bakery; and a widow from Irving, Wisconsin, who owned a valuable farm.

As long as her identity was unconfirmed, the woman's body remained on exhibition at Bayha's morgue. Over the weekend alone, multitudes of intrigued folks competed for an intimate look at her. A reporter suggested the "circus-like" atmosphere compared to entertainment like the visiting Barnum and Bailey Greatest Show on Earth in West Superior, featuring Chiko and Johanna, the giant gorillas.

Adding to the morgue's chaotic atmosphere was an odd incident that happened the following Monday, August 27, according to the *Duluth News Tribune*: "There was only one development in the Park Point mystery yesterday and that was about as mysterious as the murder itself. Yesterday afternoon a woman walked into Bayha's morgue. She picked up the bracelet of bangles and after glancing at it hurriedly, became excited, and threw it down. She then looked at the picture and became more startled and at once left the morgue. An effort was made to follow her, but she eluded her shadowers."

A follow-up note was printed a few days later: "The mysterious woman who viewed the remains Monday and betrayed such emotion and then rushed from the place has been found and her story elicited. She claims to recognize the body as that of a former friend and gave the undertaker the name and address of the parties she supposes are relatives of the corpse." Nothing more was printed on the matter.

Barnum and Bailey Greatest Show on Earth in West Superior, Wisconsin, featuring Chiko and Johanna, the giant gorillas. Courtesy of the Minnesota Historical Society Newspaper Digital Hub.

It was also reported that two unidentified men also stopped by the morgue to relate their first-hand encounter with the murder victim. They had apparently been on the same Minnesota Point streetcar Tuesday night with Branthurst, Anderson, and Sisk. One of the men recalled the small group on the streetcar making light conversation. He had taken notice of the unknown woman's jewelry. Jokingly, he remembered remarking aloud, "We might hold that woman up on the Point, and get that bracelet; we could sell it and get enough money to buy plenty of booze."[3] Both men agreed it was the same bracelet worn by the same woman who lay before them.

The first promising lead on the woman's killer was offered by George Free, a Duluth contractor. He claimed to have met her three weeks earlier with an acquaintance, a Mr. Cummings from Illinois. The couple was visiting Duluth with no known purpose. Free recalled her brown dress matched the same worn by the unknown victim in the morgue. Her companion was described as "thick set and stoutly built, about forty-five years old. His hair and beard were sprinkled with grey."

According to Free, Cummings told him he had left his wife after a quarrel in Chicago and met up in New Orleans with this woman, who he was passing off as his wife. The word on the street was that Cummings boasted of "doing" a woman of large sums of money. She remained in Duluth for a week before abruptly leaving while Cummings was out.

Within a few days, Cummings also parted, but not before requesting his boarding house landlord tell no one where he was heading. Upon a credible tip given to the detectives, Cummings was tracked down the following week in Michigan. He was found with the woman in question. The murder case had gone cold once again.

By Sunday, August 26, another sensation captured the attention of Duluth citizens. At seven thirty a.m., a newspaper boy noticed the body of a man washed up the lake shore side of Minnesota Point about a half mile from the canal. The police were notified immediately, and Detective Hayden and Coroner Eklund were "soon on the spot." Evidently, the decomposed body had been in the water for some time, as the surf's unrelenting pounding left his features nearly unrecognizable. The man's hands were tied with his handkerchief, and his feet were bound with his necktie, which led Hayden to speculate murder.

Hayden put forth that the man might be the same individual seen with the woman who was murdered the previous week. The body was moved to Durkan's morgue, located on Second Avenue West. Within a few hours, two boarders from the fashionable Merchant's Hotel on West Superior Street identified the remains as that of fellow lodger Joseph McNamee, thirty, of Topeka, Kansas. He had disappeared on August 15, leaving his luggage behind. They theorized he had skipped out on paying his hotel bill.

Those acquainted with McNamee, who had arrived in Duluth on May 25, believed he sought the north shore as a restorative elixir for his broken heart and dependency upon the bottle, which ultimately left him nearly destitute. Immediately, local newspapers shifted the cause of McNamee's death from possible murder to suicide. His brother P.A. McNamee, also of Topeka, refuted the latter claim, stating Joseph was neither despondent nor lacked funds, as he was a prosperous commission merchant. He conjectured that Joseph was dispatched for his money.

Despite midday temperatures reaching a monthly high of ninety degrees, Duluthians by the droves wasted little time in visiting Durkan's morgue to see McNamee's battered body and then heading over to Bayha's morgue to view the bludgeoned woman. Whether a connection existed at all between the two dead individuals only added to the mounting whodunit.

ᴵE DULUTH EVENING HERᴬ

SOMEONE TO BLAME

The Steamer Bruno Runs Onto the
Old Dyke With Fatal
Results.

Fred Gettling is Caught in the Screw
and Horribly Man-
gled.

An Investigation is Needed and has
Already Been De-
manded.

The expected has happened in the
Duluth harbor and it is only a wonder
that a number of people are not dead
this morning and a number of homes
desolated instead of the one terrible

Newspaper account of the steamer N.H. Bruno fatal mishap. Courtesy of the Minnesota Historical Society Newspaper Digital Hub.

O-AT-KA BEACH SUMMERTIME CALAMITIES

As a favorite summertime recreation spot, O-at-ka Beach welcomed throngs of Duluthians and out-of-town visitors. The destination was so popular that excursion boats left the Duluth docks every hour starting at nine a.m. to accommodate the numerous pleasure-seekers. As with any large gathering place, unfortunate incidents transpired. Such was the case over the span of several days in July 1892.

On Thursday evening, July 14, it was reported that teenager Mabel White was accidentally shot by a boy named Bemis. Apparently, they were part of a group of youngsters picnicking at O-at-ka Beach. While walking on the shore, Bemis took out a .32 caliber revolver and "began fooling with it." The weapon discharged and White was struck in the right breast with the bullet penetrating her lung. Immediately she was transported to her home in town and a physician was summoned. He was unable to locate the bullet, believing it may have passed through the lung and lodged in the back. Fortunately, White recovered and led a fulfilling life.

Several days after the incident, on a warm Sunday afternoon, July 17, with temperatures reaching eighty-two degrees, the little ferry steamer *N.H. Bruno* left the St. Paul and Duluth slip in St. Louis Bay at three p.m. bound for O-at-ka Beach. Overloaded with nearly one-hundred pleasure-seekers, the craft exceeded its license of up to seventy-five passengers.

With Captain C.H. Cameron collecting fares, John Daniels, ship manager and engineer, took the wheel. He admitted it was the first time he had ever attempted to navigate the steamer through the "gap" or channel across an old sunken dike. Realizing the boat would not have sufficient clearance, he tried to change course, but it was too late. Without warning, *Bruno* struck the dike and crossed over, plunging the bow into the deep water.

Duluth patrol wagon, ca. 1890. Courtesy of the Duluth Public Library, Duluth, Minnesota.

The violent shock threw several passengers, including Fred W. Gettling, a thirty-three-year-old from Marquette, Michigan, overboard. The wholesale cigar salesman was in town on business and decided to treat himself to an afternoon at the beach. Falling off the vessel near the stern, Gettling came into contact with the whirling propeller and was horribly mangled with "his ribs being literally torn from his spine and one leg frightfully jammed." No one else was injured.

Coming to the rescue, the tug *Lida* found the poor man clinging on a portion of the dike that was sticking out of the water. He was taken aboard and conveyed to the Northern Pacific dock, where he was then transported by a horse-drawn patrol wagon to St. Mary's Hospital. Sadly, there was little that could be done for Gettling, who died within a few hours.

Following the dreadful calamity, a formal inquest was held. Cameron admitted that *Bruno* was "very cranky and liable to career to a great extent." The two men were found negligent, and their licenses were revoked.

Sources: "A Distressing Accident," *Duluth Evening Herald,* July 15, 1892, 8; "Someone To Blame," *Duluth Evening Herald,* July 18, 1893, 5; "Killed by a Propeller," *St. Paul Daily Globe,* July 18, 1892, 5; and "Action is Taken," *Duluth Evening Herald,* July 26, 1892, 1.

Two days later, on Tuesday afternoon, August 28, a policeman discovered the black hat described by Branthurst in some dregs about twenty feet from where the woman's body was placed. The lace-trimmed headpiece contained an illegible dealer's mark on a small slip of cloth sewn to the interior lining. The bedraggled hat, sodden and crusted with sand, "showed signs of being a very tasty piece of millinery."

At police headquarters, the article was left to dry overnight in hope that the dealer's mark would prove visible in the morning. Authorities were then able to discern "Rue de La Paix, H.W. Virose, Paris." Feeling there might be more clues left on the beach, the police returned in the afternoon with pitchforks in hand, earnestly searching the sand in the hope of revealing the dead woman's handbag. Only blisters and frustration surfaced for the tired officers bent on solving the case.

On Thursday, August 30, McNamee was buried. Coroner Eklund decreed his death came by drowning. He gave no opinion as to whether it was suicide or murder or that his death was connected in any way to the body of the woman discovered nine days earlier on O-at-ka Beach.

The following day, August 31, at four p.m., Eklund held an inquiry regarding the dead woman. Testimony was taken from the doctors who conducted the postmortem. The jury decided that the woman came to her death from injuries to the head "inflicted feloniously" by some unknown weapon in the hands of an unknown person. The *Duluth News Tribune* headline flatly stated, "Coroner's Jury Finds the Mysterious Woman is Dead."

The time had come to properly bury the unidentified victim, considering the corpse's state of decomposition. For the past many days, she had lain as a curiosity to the public numbering in the hundreds, if not a thousand or more. Another

A picnic on Minnesota Point, Duluth, Minnesota, ca. 1895. Courtesy of the University of Minnesota Duluth, Kathryn A. Martin Library, Northeast Minnesota Historical Collections.

headline, "She is Still Dead," summarized the chilling riddle to everyone concerned, from the police who followed up on scores of fruitless leads, to the unnerved locals who desired justice for the heinous crime committed in their own backyard.[4]

Her burial was a simple affair, held on Sunday, September 2, at Forest Hill Cemetery in Duluth. At her graveside, with temperatures in the sixties, stood a few staff members from Bayha's morgue and a representative from the police department. Only a few weeks earlier, in mid-August, a black bear had been shot

in the same unfenced cemetery while reportedly "cavorting among the graves." As if in a strange and prophetic coincidence, a dead bear had washed ashore on Minnesota Point shortly before the discovery of the woman's body. A newspaper quipped, "The next thing, some young lady down there will get hugged to death."

Little coverage was given to her interment, as the day before a firestorm had devastated the community of Hinckley, Minnesota, nearly seventy miles south of Duluth. Over

200,000 acres burned, and more than 400 lives were lost—the makings of front-page news for weeks to come. The woman who was about to be buried had become "old news."

Under a hazy, smoke-filled sky, a brisk, southerly wind met those gathered to pay their final respects as her plain pine coffin, lacking decoration or inscription, was lowered into an unmarked grave. Her slayer could now let out a deep sigh of relief, as the ground concealed the threat of her identification in its dark, eternal silence.

CHAPTER THREE
Identified at Last

Several days following the burial of the slain woman, Detective Benson played a hunch and went to Minneapolis. He carried with him several large broadsides that provided a description of the victim and were illustrated with grisly photographs of her taken by Carl Thiel two weeks earlier. Benson felt incredibly fortunate that circumstances in the past week had delayed his journey. Originally he was to take the St. Paul & Duluth limited train on September 1, the same day as the great Hinckley firestorm, but the printer did not have the posters ready in time.

Had Benson been on that train with its 125 passengers, he might have perished that horrible day. As the locomotive neared Hinckley, the engine and its seven cars were soon ablaze. Surrounding them was an unimaginable inferno with flames reaching more than four miles into the sky. The intense heat and dire situation called for heroic actions. The train's engineers, James Root, William Best, and Edward Barry, backed the train up five miles to a marshy swamp named Skunk Lake. Most, if not all, of the passengers would surely have died otherwise.

Many survived by taking refuge in the murky water as the roiling funnel of fire swept past.

Upon arriving in Minneapolis, known as the greatest flour and lumber market in the world, Benson sought and received the cooperation of his colleagues. The broadsides were soon placed in the windows of several prominent stores. An official appeal was made requesting that anyone who recognized the woman or knew anything of her should come forward. Benson figured that in the city of 190,000 surely at least one individual would recognize the woman.

The response was overwhelming. Hundreds of people called at police headquarters to learn more about the woman or to share information. One man, Daniel Haller, thought that the photograph of the dead woman resembled his own wife. She had left him the previous May, intending to return to her parents in Michigan. Haller believed her route home would have taken her through Duluth. His assertion was dismissed as his wife did not quite resemble the victim.

St. Cloud, Minnesota, Chief of Police James McKelvey was of the strong opinion that the woman was none other than a Mrs. Belle Fassbender, who came to his city from the Duluth area with her husband a year or two earlier. They had opened a restaurant, quarreled, and separated after a "number of sensational episodes." Her husband felt she had become a "reckless woman" after she left. McKelvey thought the description of the jewelry found on the woman closely matched that of Fassbender and wondered if she was the woman violently dispatched in Duluth.

The most convincing identification happened on Friday, September 7. Mrs. Anna Gow, who operated a boarding house on 16th Street North, Minneapolis, immediately recognized the woman and her personal effects featured in the postmortem photographs. Gow told authorities that the woman was one of her former residents, a respectable Norwegian-American named Lena Olson—noteworthy considering there were sixteen other Lena Olsons living in the Mill City at that time.[5]

The next morning, Lena's younger sister, Lizzie, who was employed by a wealthy family on Lake Minnetonka, met with Benson in Minneapolis. Upon reviewing the broadsides and discussing the case, Lizzie was convinced the murdered woman was none other than her sister who also worked as a servant. Benson and Olson left together that afternoon by train bound for Duluth. Their objective was to establish beyond any question of a doubt the identity of the woman killed at O-at-ka Beach.

Arriving in Duluth midevening, Saturday, September 8, Olson was shown the items not buried with the victim. With several pairs of anxious eyes upon her, she inspected the clothing and jewelry. Immediately Olson recognized each item as having belonged to her deceased sister. The Egyptian brooch was given to Lena by a former Minneapolis employer, Mrs. Agnes Hull. The embroidered trim on the skirt was done by brother Erick's wife, Mary. The telling silver bracelet with its dozen bangles was a gift from fellow residents at Gow's boarding house.[6]

Convinced that Olson was confident in her identification of the sundry items, Benson and his fellow officers decided to have undertaker Bayha exhume the woman's remains the next afternoon.[7] Although the body was in a decrepit state upon viewing, Olson pronounced positively it was her older sister, thirty-two-year-old Lena, thus solving the mystery.

Lena's short life had been relatively uneventful until her final fateful days. She was born Olena P. Olson on June 23, 1862, in a Norwegian immigrant enclave, Stoughton, Dane County, Wisconsin. Her parents, Peter and Bertha, and their eight-year-old son Andrew, had immigrated the year before from the Krogen farm in Luster, Vestland County, Norway, a picturesque area in the southwest of the country featuring fjords, waterfalls, mountains, and valleys. By 1863, the family had relocated to Decorah, Iowa. Bertha passed away in 1868, leaving behind four children: Andrew (fifteen), Olena "Lena" (five), Erick (four), and infant Elizabeth "Lizzie." Their father remarried two years later.

Like so many other children of immigrants, Lena possessed only an elementary education. By her later teenage years, she found work as a household employee—"a servant girl," otherwise known as a domestic. A typical day in a seven-day work week started by six a.m., with duties that included lighting fires, sweeping floors, polishing silver and brass, preparing meals, washing clothes, washing dishes, ironing clothes, and cleaning the house. The days were long and stretched well into the evening. Servants were given a half day off each week and paid on average $10–12 per week.

Lena had been working in Minneapolis for the past ten years or so. According to Lizzie, she had always been employed by "good families and has been well liked." But her demise in Duluth baffled everyone. In Lizzie's estimation, addressing her sister's killer would have to wait following a proper burial in Minneapolis. Before departing by train with the body on Monday, September 10, Lizzie voiced her dissatisfaction with the pine box coffin in which she found the remains of her sister.

LENA OLSON.

Lena Olson, ca. 1894. Courtesy of the University of Minnesota Duluth, Kathryn A. Martin Library, Northeast Minnesota Historical Collections.

A sketch of a Victorian-era undertaker, ca. 1895. Courtesy of the Minnesota Historical Society Newspaper Digital Hub.

Benson agreed to purchase a more presentable $59 casket on her behalf. Years later, he groused that she never paid him back.

The funeral of Lena Olson took place at nine a.m. on Wednesday, September 12, at Trinity Norwegian Church located at Tenth Avenue South and Fourth Street in Minneapolis. Rev. M. Falk Gjertsen performed the services. Lena was re-interred in an unmarked grave at the Lakewood Cemetery in Minneapolis.[8]

Others resting in the row included Adolph Heanz, who was killed in a train accident, and James H. Allen, a victim of typhoid fever. Sgt. Charles Whitehead, a police officer from

Butte, Montana, also was buried there. Whitehead was acting as special security for a traveling exhibit featuring the statue known as *Justice*, which was cast out of pure silver for the World's Columbian Exposition in 1893. On his day off, September 9, 1894, Whitehead joined other boaters on Lake Minnetonka. He fell overboard and drowned. His body was not recovered and buried for another six days.

Family and friends of Lena Olson had little doubt that the person who committed the terrible crime was none other than a smooth-talking Englishman known as Albert A. Austin who beguiled Lena months earlier.

Final resting place of Lena Olson, Lakewood Cemetery, Minneapolis, Minnesota. Courtesy of Evelyn Hoover, Northfield, Minnesota.

Lizzie said, "Lena told us she was going to marry him, but we advised her to have nothing to do with him. I never liked his looks. He acted in a sneaking manner and always evaded a person's eyes." She added, "When Lena went away, she said she was going to South Dakota to consult my brother [Erick] there before she got married. That was the last we saw of her."

Lena Olson had first encountered the mysterious Austin the previous April. Her employer, Matilda Clay, operated an employment agency in Minneapolis that hired out women for domestic services. Austin stopped in and inquired about hiring a trustworthy housekeeper. She described him as a "fine looking man, who was quiet in manner, and very gentlemanly."[9]

Austin represented himself as a man of means who originally hailed from England. For a while he lived in New York state, then settled in Los Angeles, where he owned several properties. He intimated that he was widowed and needed help with his twelve-year-old daughter. Clay introduced Olson to him, and their business relationship quickly drifted to a romantic one. He simply "wormed himself into the confidence of the woman," one newspaper noted. While keeping company with Olson, Austin told her that he was living in St. Paul but did not specify any particular location.

The couple enjoyed spending their evenings playing cards at Thea Larson's dressmaking parlor located at 721 Hennepin Avenue. Larson was a close friend and sometimes roommate of Olson. Joining them on occasion were Lizzie and a friend, Emma Olson, no relation, who also worked as a domestic in the same house where Lena was employed. Lizzie remarked that Austin was "very clever with cards."

She described him as dark-complected, between forty and forty-five years of age, six feet tall, and weighing 170 pounds. He wore a heavy, black mustache and thick side whiskers. His dark hair, tinged with gray, was combed, oiled, and pasted down over his forehead. His upper eyelids drooped. His hands were large and white, and the backs of them were covered with hair. He had a very prominent nose, a broad, high forehead, and his face tapered to a point at the chin. Austin always wore a black stiff hat. Whenever he appeared, he wore a dirty, gray suit of clothes.

In a *St. Paul Daily Globe* interview, Clay related that Austin was a "smooth-tongued fellow," and despite his age managed to win the woman's heart. "She became infatuated with him, and the two met at various places almost every night. On some occasions he waited for her at the West Hotel, where he claimed he was a guest. This sort of thing ran along all summer, and in spite of what Lena's friends said to her concerning Austin and his pretensions, she continued seeing him."

By July, Austin asked Olson to marry him, and she consented. In the ensuing weeks, Olson announced to family and friends that she intended to marry, and no one could dissuade her from what they felt was clearly a poor decision. It was said of Olson that she was a most determined woman, and once she had made up her mind, nothing could turn her.

Gow, who operated the boarding house on 16th Street North where Olson occasionally resided when out of work, was interviewed at length by the *Minneapolis Tribune*. To her, the greatest mystery of the girl's murder was the fact that she allowed any man to gain such influence over her as Austin had. She says Lena had never been known to go anywhere with a man and always seemed a little frightened if one talked to her very much. She was a young woman of excellent morals. Gow further explained:

> *The boys who boarded with me, often tried to get Lena to go out with them in the evening, but she never would. Once in a while she would go with my husband to some entertainment when I could not go with them, but never anyone else. But that man [Austin] in some way made her do as he wished, though she never would follow the advice of anyone before. She was*

very headstrong. When I told her she was not doing right in going with this man she would not listen. She did promise me, though, after I had done a lot of talking, that should her brother [Erick] at Edgerton [South Dakota], where she told me she was going, object to her marrying the man, that she would not go against his wishes.

I never saw Austin by daylight but once, and that was the day he came with a drayman to get Lena's trunks. He was one of these smooth fellows that are always talking. He thought it was wrong for a woman to work as hard as I do, and said that when Lena married him she would never have to do a bit of work. The day Lena left here she cried as she said goodbye to me and seemed unhappy. When she left the house Saturday afternoon, she told me, when I questioned her, that she was not going to draw her money out of the bank, and when she returned she told me she had.

Lena was not fond of jewelry, but she was of good clothes. She never bought a dress that cost her less than $2 or $3 a yard, and she had the handsomest underwear I ever saw. Her hats always cost her $10 and $12 apiece, and she had elegant wraps for the various seasons. In the pasteboard box which she took she had two silk waists which cost her $12 each. She was not even pretty, and still she believed Austin when he would tell her that she was. She fairly worshiped him, but for all that I don't think she trusted him; that is, I think she was always a little afraid of him.

Lena and her sister Lizzie was not as fond of each other as some sisters are, and Lena never told Lizzie any of her affairs. The first Lizzie knew any of Austin was when Lena told her that she was going to their brother and he was going, too, and was going to marry her. Lizzie tried to convince Lena that this man never meant to marry her, but she would not listen. Lena had

once been engaged to a Frenchman, who died, and wore a plain
gold ring which he had given her, but no other jewelry excepting
a silver friendship ring, which I think Austin gave her, and her
watch, which was worth $45. I wish I could have seen that man
hanged for killing that poor girl.

Olson let on that she was leaving on Monday, August 20, for South Dakota, where she planned to visit her brother Erick, a hotel proprietor, and solicit his advice about her upcoming marriage. Austin would follow her in a couple of days. Shortly before departing, Olson withdrew her life savings from the bank. Speculation on the amount ran as high as $1,000, a large sum accumulated in the last dozen years by living prudently.[10] For whatever reason before leaving, Olson entrusted at least $400 to her employer, Clay.

Around noon, two St. Paul draymen hired by Austin arrived at Gow's to pick up Olson's two trunks and deliver them to St. Paul's Union Depot. A Minneapolis drayman later remarked that he voiced his displeasure at the men working on the west side of the river. One of the men bellowed back that they were getting "well paid for their job."

Unbeknownst to all, after leaving Gow's boarding house, Austin and Olson were secretly married in St. Paul by the Rev. William E. Barker at Philadelphia Baptist Church. His wife and another woman served as witnesses. Three years later, in September 1897, Barker's recollections of the ceremony were published in the *Duluth Evening Herald*:

At the time the murder was reported in the daily papers, I failed
to identify the names, not, of course dreaming that I had ever

known anything of the parties; and, in fact, paying little or no attention to the account. When I did at length see some reference to the tragedy that arrested my serious attention, the names appeared to be somewhat familiar, and at once on consulting my record, the shocking truth dawned upon me.

Albert Austin, of St. Paul and Lena Olson, of Minneapolis, were by me united in marriage in St. Paul, August 20, 1894. In my own journal I find in connection with the record of the marriage this memorandum: "Parties intending to take the evening train for Duluth, en route for Los Angeles, Cal." In view of all the circumstances in the case, there can be no doubt of the identity of these parties with those concerned in the Duluth tragedy which occurred only three or four days later.

He was a man about forty-five years of age, of pleasant speech and good bearing, and stated that he had been engaged in grain speculation in St. Paul for some time previous. She was a modest appearing young woman, apparently from thirty to thirty-five years old, with a frank open countenance, and a manner which plainly indicated sincerity of purpose.

On speaking with them both, as I often do on such occasion, of the importance of together leading a Christian life, she told me with tearful eyes and the utmost apparent sincerity of voice and manner, that she had been brought up in the Lutheran church, that she felt she had not always lived as a true Christian should, but that it was her desire to be such, and that she knew it was the only right way to live.

I relate these facts in the hope that they may prove to be of some satisfaction, even at this late date, to relatives and friends. [11]

Barker's journal entry was indeed telling, but unfortunately forgotten for possible use at the time of the initial investigation.

By mid-September 1894, once it became known that Austin was the prime suspect in the murder of Olson, a clerk at the Merchant's Hotel, 310 East Superior Street, Duluth, made a strong connection. While looking over the hotel's register, he discovered that on Tuesday, August 21, the newlyweds had been guests. Austin signed for room nineteen as "A. Austin and Wife, St. Paul."

The clerk remembered they came in before breakfast, ate, registered, and then left to take in the sights. Neither of them had any baggage, which he thought was a little peculiar. The Austins returned to the hotel for dinner, spent the afternoon away, and then came back for an early supper. That was the last time the clerk noticed them. Another clerk recalled that around 10:30 that night, Austin came in alone, paid the bill for the single day, and departed. The following morning, August 22, Guy Browning found Olson's body on O-at-ka Beach.

In order to create an alibi for himself, Austin called upon Emma Olson in the coming days. She had not heard yet of the murder that took place in Duluth nor made any connection to Austin, considering that he and Lena had made it known their intention was to visit South Dakota, not Minnesota's north shore. It puzzled her that Lena was not with him. "I want to talk with you about Lena," Austin said. He then invited her to walk with him in the park. Olson declined, so he told her all he had to say.

"Lena and I have had a little trouble, and Lena has gone to live with her brother in Edgerton, South Dakota. Lena will never write to any of her friends, and they will never see her again. I am going to England for a few months, after which I shall return to my home in Los Angeles." The conversation and

Marriage license between Albert A. Austin and Lena Olson, August 20, 1894.
Courtesy of Ramsey County Public Health, Vital Records (Marriage Records).

NUPTIALS NAUGHT?

The marriage story between Albert A. Austin and Lena Olson was later scoffed at by Duluth detective Bob Benson. "There is absolutely no foundation to such a statement; and I will tell you why." Benson claimed that Mrs. Gow, Lizzie Olson, and another claimed Olson and Austin went to Duluth because he had $500 to collect there. The couple's intention was then to journey to South Dakota, where Olson sought her brother's advice on her pending marriage.

Benson also asserted that Olson had retained $500 of her life savings and the money was on her person when visiting Duluth. Interestingly, no one apparently checked with Ramsey County to see whether a marriage license for Austin and Olson existed. In 2020, the author secured a facsimile of the record, thus proving that Rev. William E. Barker did indeed marry the couple as he truthfully stated in the press.

Lizzie Olson refuted Benson's claim that she knew of her sister heading to Duluth with Austin. According to her statement, Olson believed Benson made that up, and furthermore, "there was not a soul [who] knew of Lena's departure with her murderer until after her body was found."

Sources: "Duluth Story Denied," *Minneapolis Journal*, September 3, 1897, 6; and "Lena Olson Not Married," *Duluth News Tribune*, September 29, 1897, 4.

Austin's emphatic tone struck Olson as strange. With no more to say, Austin turned around and left. She never saw him again.

Following up on the most credible clues and eyewitness accounts, the sleuthing Detective Benson believed the man seen with Lena Olson the day of the murder tallied in description with the one given of Austin. Finding her missing trunks might lead the authorities to the elusive killer. A notice stating "Two Draymen Wanted" was placed by Benson in the newspapers as he sought the identities of the St. Paul men who picked up Olson's baggage from Gow's residence. He offered a slice of reward upon Austin's arrest, but to no avail. The draymen and Austin could not be traced, much to the chagrin of the detective. Also odd was that no one in Minneapolis knew where Austin roomed or boarded.

The public outcry to catch Austin was heard loud and clear by Minnesota Gov. Knute Nelson, a Norwegian-American like Olson. On September 18, 1894, the state offered a reward of $250 for the arrest and conviction of the murderer. On October 5, the St. Louis County board of commissioners matched the reward in response to a petition submitted on October 1 by thirty-three county residents.

With a sizable apprehension war chest, Duluth Chief of Police Harry Armstrong then forwarded hundreds of reward circulars across the country: "$500 Reward! Wanted for Murder! One A.A. Austin." The poster contained Lizzie's description of the mysterious Englishman, but not his likeness. An added descriptive note surmised, "He is a good talker. Will be liable to be found among 'tin-horn' gamblers." The nationwide manhunt for Austin was underway.

$500 REWARD

Wanted for Murder
ONE A. A. AUSTIN,
whose description is as follows:

About 6 ft. high, erect build, 40 to 45 years of age, wei
190 lbs.; dark sallow complexion, prominent nose, dark ey
long face; when last seen wore a medium-sized black mo
tache sprinkled with grey, sideburns the same; hair black
shiny, combed well down over the forehead; would be pa
bald in front if hair was combed back; forehead high
broad, with a face tapering to the chin, his upper eye
hung down, or folded over showing a surplus of skin; h
black and thick on back of hands. He wore a dirty g
suit of clothes, and is a good talker. Will be liable to
found among "tin-horn" gamblers.

HISTORY OF HIS CRIME.

In March, 1894, Austin made his appearance in Minneapolis, Minn., where he went to an empl
office and represented himself as a well-to-do widower from Los Angeles, Cal., that he had a daugh
years old and was looking for a trustworthy housekeeper; money no object; to the right woman;
introduced to Lena Olson, a very highly respected servant girl of that city, and who had out of hard
wages saved about $450 from twelve years work. Austin, as we believe him to be, a professional robb
murderer, set about at once to obtain the money, and he on the 21st of August, 1894, decoyed Miss O
this city on promise of marriage, took her to an isolated place on the shore of Lake Superior, clu
until she was unconscious, and with a large slob knocks her skull in, robbed her of her hard earned
and left this city the same night. There will be no question of convicting if we can get him. The s
Minnesota offers $250 and the Lewis County offers $250, making a total of $500 for his arrest.

Austin claims to be originally from England, and lived for some time in New York state.
address all information to:

H. R. ARMSTRONG, Chief of Police
DULUTH, MIN

And will send officers at once with requisition papers.

Reward circular issued for suspected murderer A.A. Austin, 1894. Courtesy of Worthpoint.com.

CHAPTER FOUR
Pursuit of Suspects

A round the same time Albert A. Austin first appeared in Minneapolis, the city of Duluth appointed Harry R. Armstrong chief of police on March 14, 1894. Having served for six years as a sheriff's deputy, Armstrong was known as an able administrator who was efficient and interested in the latest developments in police work. Within a year's time, he would significantly reduce crime in Zenith City, gain the trust and confidence of its citizens, and enjoy the respect of his men.

Shortly after Armstrong became chief, he rehired thirty-one-year-old Robert "Bob" Benson as the senior detective to work alongside the department's only other detective, thirty-year-old Tom Hayden. Within five months, the senior sleuth would lead the investigation of the Lena Olson murder. Both men had previously worked together on the force from 1887 to 1890, when Benson resigned or was dismissed, as some speculated, and started a private detective agency.

Benson first landed in Duluth around 1881, "fresh from the cranberry swamps of Michigan, somewhat green and unsophisticated."[12] Initially, he was employed as a "setter" in a local sawmill. In 1885, Benson joined the police force as a patrolman,

Members of the Duluth Police Department, 1889. Detective Bob Benson, 1st row—3rd from left; Detective Tom Hayden, 2nd row—2nd from left. Courtesy of the University of Minnesota Duluth, Kathryn A. Martin Library, Northeast Minnesota Historical Collections.

and by 1888 was promoted to detective. His partner, the strapping and exceptionally clever and likeable Hayden, stood six foot three and weighed nearly 240 pounds. Like Benson, he started out as a patrolman in 1887 and was made detective on June 1, 1890, after Benson left the department.

Both men were involved in the July 6, 1889, labor strike and ensuing riot in Duluth's west end. After a gun battle between the police and a large mob, three men lay dead and at least thirty injured. Hayden was shot in his right forearm, and Benson narrowly missed death when a bullet grazed his scalp. Grateful citizens bestowed gold medals on the officers who distinguished themselves by individual acts of bravery.

Yet, Benson's heroics that day did not sit well with some, particularly in the west end of town. One of the men killed in the confrontation was striker Edward Johnson, twenty-two, who had only arrived in Duluth from Michigan six days earlier. Apparently, he had run forward to throw stones at the police. Johnson then retreated nearly a block when Benson leveled his rifle and shot him through the head.

On the morning of July 9, Benson received a letter without a signature. The writer addressed him as "Bob Benson, the slayer of Johnson," and threatened death to the detective within the month, saying he would "either be shot with a revolver or clubbed to death." Duluth's Mayor John Sutphin also received a foreboding epistle, misspellings and all: "Yure days are few, now, so we rite you these few lines so you can git redy to die we mean bisness, so god help you. we are after that Benson, to. We want his scalp." The letter was signed "Striker." Although nothing came out of the bloodthirsty, anonymous letters, Benson's reputation never fully recovered from the perceived notion that he killed Johnson in cold blood.

To most Duluthians, however, Benson was seen as a genial, hard-boiled detective, capable of handling the toughs, vagabonds, and "plug uglies" about. His methods, crude by modern standards, were acceptable in its day. Benson was known to choke, grab, or punch to subdue a lawbreaker. On one occasion he chased three burglars down a street, firing his revolver three times while shouting at them to stop. He was sued in court for false imprisonment and lambasted for his overreach of authority. It was said of him, "While in the police force, he developed nerve and cheek and acquired a vocabulary of abuse that would turn a fishwife green with envy."

Results counted, however, and Benson and Hayden delivered. The duo made a strong team, and criminals knew to watch their step in the port city. Their work favorably compared to that of departments containing two and three times the number of men. Under Armstrong's leadership at the big brick Central Station, Duluth had never before witnessed less frequent crime.

It is worth noting that one of the patrolmen under Chief Armstrong, Henry Threadcroft (often spelled Threadcraft) was most likely Duluth's first Black officer. Although his tenure with the department was brief, he has been all but forgotten in the annals of Duluth's history. Threadcroft joined the force in June 1893. In a clipping from 1895, he was briefly mentioned: "Patrolman Henry Threadcroft, deserves special mention. There is not a man on the force more attentive to duty, and whenever he has been transferred from his beat, which is on Fourth Street, there is sure to be a delegation of merchants waiting on the chief to ask that he be put back." In October 1898, Threadcroft was dismissed for apparently "sassing" the mayor, Henry Truelsen.

Newspaper readers were regularly entertained by stories of the police station's operational success and its working environment, deemed "a little world unto itself." A red light over the front entrance read "Police Headquarters," but perhaps it should also have said in smaller letters "Museum of Macabre." Armstrong used a large case to display his collection of gruesome relics of crimes committed throughout Duluth's history as well as items he picked up from across the country.

Some of the relics, such as revolvers, skulls, or bits of hangman's rope, dated to the early years of the department. After Lena Olson was murdered, the four-foot-long oak stick used to fracture her skull became the most regarded artifact in the museum. Other objects included a knife used by a villain who "tried to cut a lung out of Bob Benson" in January 1887. The plucky, wounded officer was able to bring in his assailant, but the charge against him was later dismissed for some unknown reason. Bark from a tree where a man was lynched, wires, laudanum, twisted leather belts, and barbershop razors adorned with dried blood illustrated the suicide exhibit. Rounding out the dark side of human nature was a pickled ear bitten off by a ruffian who was sentenced to three years in prison to cure him of his gnawing habit.

Armstrong insisted on the latest improvements in solving crimes, and one of the most important instruments of the day was the compilation of criminal photographs, known as a rogues' gallery. His first act as police chief was to contact the

Stillwater State Prison to secure mugshots of all current and former incarcerated convicts, including the Younger brothers Bob, Cole, and Jim. They were captured after a failed attempt to rob a Northfield, Minnesota, bank in 1876. Their fellow conspirators, Frank and Jesse James, eluded authorities.

The value in gallery books was that no person photographed could distort his face to make any features unrecognizable. Likewise, a person could not change the shape of his nose, his chin, or the general outline of their head. Most importantly, ears were a discernible feature in identification, as no ears in the world compare exactly.

When a reporter toured the detectives' room in 1895, Armstrong took great pride in explaining how the well-stocked rogues' gallery worked as an incalculable benefit particularly to Benson and Hayden. A random photograph was selected:

> *"Who is this, chief?" The chief looked at the number on the photographs and then took down a large book. "That," said he, after he had found the corresponding number in the book and read the accompanying description, "is Mamie Thompson. She is a house thief, and is probably the same woman who was here a couple of years ago. She has been operating in several cities, generally representing herself as a domestic and doing some skillful work in robbing houses."*

Although the Duluth authorities did not have a mugshot of Austin in their gallery, they needed to act quickly in order to track him down. The enticing $500 advertised on the reward poster would surely interest parties from coast to coast. Armstrong believed that he and his intrepid sleuths would soon have their man and was ready for the deluge of possible suspects put forth. The first promising lead took only a matter of days.

Duluth City Detective Robert "Bob" Benson, ca. 1895. Courtesy of the University of Minnesota Duluth, Kathryn A. Martin Library, Northeast Minnesota Historical Collections.

After the circular for Austin was distributed nationwide, numerous suspects emerged. One blurb from the *Duluth Evening Herald* stated, "Another Austin has been found, this last one being reported at Bushnell, Illinois. The authorities holding him were instructed to send a photograph of the suspect. Chief Armstrong will give these photos a special shelf in the rogues' gallery and will mark them A.P.A.—'all presumed Austins.'" This suspect proved a false lead.

The Alpena, South Dakota, Suspect

In the days following Lena Olson's burial in Minneapolis, Benson received a plausible tip from the sheriff of Alpena,

South Dakota, regarding A.A. Austin's whereabouts. "I started out at once. On reaching Alpena the sheriff told me the following story: He was driving along the road about five miles from Alpena one day going to visit a friend in the country. He stopped at a farmhouse to inquire [about] the way. The man he saw replied that he could not direct the sheriff, as he had just come from Duluth and was a stranger. The sheriff asked him if he was well acquainted in Duluth. 'No,' he replied. 'I was only there a short time. I used to live in Minneapolis.'"

The stranger's response reminded the sheriff of the recent Olson murder in Duluth, and he felt the man more than met the description of Austin. The sheriff then asked him if he had heard of the murder. At this point, the man remained silent and walked away. Benson added, "I drove out with the sheriff to see the fellow and found he was not the man. He tallied in a general way with the description of Austin, but in some particulars he differed widely. His name was Larson, and he was living there with his aunt. He came to Alpena, July 17, so that fixes his innocence, as Austin was in Duluth, August 21."

The Spring Valley, Illinois, Suspect

An October 22, 1894, *The Duluth Evening Herald* headline trumpeted: "Austin is Captured. Man arrested at Spring Valley, Illinois, is in all probability the Murderer of Lena Olson." In the early afternoon the day before, Armstrong received a telegram from the Spring Valley chief of police Michael Hicks, who thought he had apprehended the notorious Austin. The man in question was forty-four-year-old George Smalley, a former hotel and saloon keeper from Cambridge City, Illinois.

A few days prior, Hicks had received the reward circular. The description of Austin was nearly identical to Smalley, who was pulled out of his hotel bed and charged with murder. Found on his person were incriminating letters and a memorandum book. Furthermore, Smalley had registered at two different hotels in the past week under aliases George C. Cooper and Fred Smalley. Armstrong telegraphed back to send photographs. Hicks responded by telegraphing the following:

Can't send you the pictures. He has letters in his possession from a woman asking him what trouble he got into at Minneapolis. ... In his memorandum book we found the name of J.E. Austin. He registered under two different names here. The letter he has shows he was in Minnesota on Aug. 21. You better send a man for him as he is trying to get out on a writ of habeas corpus. Answer quick. We have also found pictures of two Swede girls in his pocket.

With the fear of Smalley's immediate release due to habeas corpus (a person under arrest must be brought before a judge or into court, especially to secure the person's release unless lawful grounds are shown for their detention), Armstrong instructed Benson to catch the next train to northwest Illinois, ascertain if he was indeed Austin, and if so, return with him to Duluth. Before leaving, Benson wired Hicks and advised the authorities to search the suspect's boarding house for Lena Olson's two missing trunks, which had not yet been located.

Those familiar with Smalley were surprised to hear he was charged with the murder of Olson. For many years he ran his establishment in Cambridge City but had closed his business and left town due to financial difficulties the year before. Since then, his friends were unaware of his whereabouts.

To Benson's astonishment upon arriving in Spring Valley in the late afternoon on October 23, an eager crowd greeted him outside the city jail. The consensus among those present was that Smalley was innocent, but nevertheless, they were anxious to learn whether Benson agreed with them. The curious throng did not have to wait long. Although it was not recorded how Benson determined that Smalley was not Austin, the detective telegraphed Armstrong, "Not our man. Have had photograph taken. Coming at once via Chicago."

The New Orleans, Louisiana, Suspect

Less than two months later, New Orleans authorities arrested a man who went by the name of Arthur Austin. Leading up to his arrest on Monday evening, December 10, a thirtyish-year-old woman named Mrs. L. Kerran from Minneapolis registered at the Merchant's Hotel in Duluth. She spent the evening writing letters, and at eleven p.m. she handed her correspondence over to a hotel messenger to mail. One of the letters was addressed to "Arthur Austin, New Orleans, La." Within the hour, local authorities were made privy to this, and after midnight approached her directly.

Detective Hayden asked her abruptly, "Who is this Arthur Austin you wrote a letter to last night?" Kerran, described as a "grass widow" (a woman living away from her husband), and who had formerly lived in Duluth, was "shocked to learn that the police wanted to know anything about her acquaintances." Without holding back, she told Hayden that Arthur Austin was an alias; the letter recipient's real name was Charles C. Pettus. He was a prominent racetrack follower and bookmaker, who preferred, however, to be called Austin.

Kerran also confided that Pettus had in July placed an advertisement in the *Minneapolis Tribune*, "in which he stated his keen desire to become acquainted with some handsome young woman for a brief spell." She answered the advertisement and the two kept company while he attended the Hamline horse races at the state fairgrounds in St. Paul. By late August, shortly after the murder of Olson, they left together for the race circuit in the south. She returned to Minnesota, alone, several months later.

Following the new lead, Hayden and Benson conferred over Kerran's story. Although the two men had heard hundreds of stories since the murder of Olson on August 21, something was amiss about hers. Hayden recollected that on August 27, a railroad brakeman named Judd Humphrey from Omaha had approached him about a strange passenger who went by the name of C.C. Pettus. Humphrey reported that Pettus first arrived in Duluth around the time of Olson's murder. Pettus wore a mustache and beard, but when he left Duluth, his face was clean shaven, and he acted very nervous. His clothes also matched the description of Austin's attire.

Armed with these new clues, the detectives pushed forward. On Wednesday night, December 12, New Orleans chief of police Clark was telegraphed by the Duluth police to inquire if he knew anything about Pettus. Clark responded the next morning that the man was unknown to him. Wasting little time, Armstrong instructed Hayden to interview people in Minneapolis that might shed more light on the suspect.

Hayden spent Thursday morning speaking with racetrack men, but none of them knew Pettus or Arthur Austin. Then he called on Kerran, who had returned to her apartment. Hayden asked her to describe Pettus, her former male companion, and found his likeness closely matched A.A. Austin. Afterward, he knocked on a few doors in her building, questioning the neighbors, whose descriptions of Pettus also matched that of Olson's alleged slayer.

By noon the same day, Hayden telegraphed Armstrong requesting him to notify New Orleans chief of police Clark to have Pettus arrested. On Friday, December 14, Hayden again called on Kerran. She showed him letters written to her by Arthur Austin, mailed from locations that included New York, Chicago, St. Louis, Cincinnati, and other places. She also produced a photograph of him that Pettus had given her. Hayden took the photograph over to show Lizzie Olson, Lena's sister. "That's not the man," he was flatly told.

At the same moment Hayden returned the photograph to Kerran, a messenger delivered a telegram sent from Pettus to her. Hayden watched as she opened the envelope and read, "Am arrested for the murder of Lena Olson. Have spent the night in jail." She screamed, "My God! Arthur has been arrested for murder," and fainted.[13] After reviving Kerran, Hayden hurried to the police station and wired Armstrong, "The case is off. Pettus not the man. Have him released."

Following the Pettus episode, numerous false arrests occurred in the fall of 1894, including those of a swindler in California and a man in West Duluth who closely matched Austin's description. In fact, the Duluthian was twice charged for the murder. The first time he was arrested he took the matter "gracefully." However, when officers came after him the second time, he was not so cordial.

The Minneapolis, Minnesota, Suspect

During the same stretch in December as the Arthur Austin/ Pettus case in New Orleans was concluding, another development in Minneapolis offered new clues to solving the Olson murder. Duluth authorities considered that perhaps someone else besides A.A. Austin may have been responsible for the death of Olson. Hayden traveled to Minneapolis to chase down the new leads and hopefully connect another party with the crime. Benson told the press in a rather vague way that the new clues were "faint and may lead to nothing."

When asked by the press if the suspect Austin may yet be in Minneapolis, Benson replied that he did not believe so. "I can hardly say that I have much faith that anything will result of the investigation, but small things sometimes lead to important ends." Armstrong refused to state the exact nature of the clues for fear of jeopardizing the investigation or alerting the suspected party. But whispers within the department soon leaked out that efforts were being made to connect a Minneapolis man named Harry T. Hayward to the Olson murder.

On December 6, 1894, Hayward had been charged with the murder of Catherine "Kitty" Ging, twenty-nine, that took place three evenings earlier. The case that unfolded in the following months against the villainous playboy took the nation by storm. A son of a prosperous family, Hayward lived in and managed an apartment building known as the Ozark Flats, at the corner of Hennepin Avenue and 13th Street. The building was owned by his father, W.W. Hayward.

Ging, a dressmaker, also lived in the same building. He claimed he was "doing her" to gain her trust and money. What became evident was Hayward's insatiable appetite for high living, his gambling habits, and his seduction of others—some said by hypnotism. People meant little to nothing to him, only how they might help line his pockets, alive or dead, according to close associates.

Needing a henchman to carry out his nefarious crimes, Hayward turned to the simple-minded and mentally unstable Claus Blixt, the janitor for the Ozark Flats. Described as a

CLAUS A. BLIXT,
The Tool Employed by Harry T. Hayward to Carry Out His Hellish Design.

HARRY T. HAYWARD,
The Arch-Conspirator, Who for Three Months Plotted the Death of Kitty Ging.

MISS CATHERINE GING,
The Girl Who Was Murdered for Her Money About 8 O'clock Monday Evening.

Claus A. Blixt, the murderer of Catherine "Kitty" Ging, December 3, 1894. Harry T. Hayward, the mastermind behind her murder. Catherine Ging, the victim. All images are courtesy of Library of Congress, Chronicling America.

"filthy, inferior and ignorant looking specimen," the brute killed Ging by a shot to the head while the two of them were out for a carriage ride. Hayward, who had convinced Ging to make him the beneficiary on a life insurance policy, was anxious to "off-her" for a modest sum.

The similarities between the Olson and Ging murders, each woman beguiled by an unscrupulous fiend and then lured to their deaths for money, offered more than a kernel of plausibility in connecting Hayward to the crimes. In an interview, Minneapolis Police Chief Vernon Smith commented in a guarded and deliberate way:

> *The Olson case and the Ging case are greatly alike in many respects. Both were cold blooded murders in every sense of the word, and showed careful planning and scheming on the part of a villain who would stop at nothing in order to accomplish his ends. I cannot say now whether or not we ever suspected young Hayward of having any connection with the crime, but I would not be surprised to hear that other people had, in view of the Ging case.*

Blixt, who received a life sentence in prison, offered his take on the Olson murder: "All I know about that is that Lena Olson once lived at the Ozark Flats and that Harry was intimately acquainted with the person who is supposed to have gone with her to the place of her death." He added, "Hayward was the instigator of the murder of Lena Olson, just as he was of the killing of poor Catherine Ging. And he was the beneficiary of that crime as he hoped to benefit by the death of Miss Ging."

There was some truth to Blixt's assertion that Olson had at least worked at one time or another in the Ozark Flats. She lived in the neighborhood and was hired by families who resided in Hayward's building, including attorney W.E. Hale, who coincidentally, represented Hayward early on when charged with the Ging murder. It was not implausible that Hayward and Blixt, his catspaw, may have informally known Olson as she had worked in the building where they lived.

The mysterious web grew as more than one tried to place Hayward in the Duluth-Superior area at the time of the Olson

Duluth Police Headquarters, Duluth, Minnesota. Courtesy of the Duluth Public Library, Duluth, Minnesota.

CHIEF ARMSTRONG'S GHOULISH MUSEUM

One of the ghastlier relics in Duluth Police Chief Harry Armstrong's exhibit was a small, triangular section of skull removed from a victim named Matt Mattson. Sticking in the bone was a broken blade about two and half inches long, of which two inches had penetrated his brain. Accompanying this gruesome item was the matching remnant of the knife found on Mattson's killer, John Erickson.

Shortly after midnight on September 19, 1892, the two men, both Finlanders, had stepped outside the rear of Hart's Saloon located on Lake Avenue South in Duluth. Witnesses stated that no disagreement had occurred between the two purportedly sober men, yet for some unexplained reason, Erickson was offended when Mattson said goodnight to him. At which point, he plunged a knife into Mattson's head a few inches above his left ear. Another man, Matt Johnson, witnessed the assault. He exclaimed to Erickson, "You struck him with a knife!" To which Erickson replied, "Yes, and I struck him damn hard too!"

Authorities were summoned within minutes, and Erickson was soon located a short distance away and arrested. A police officer found a knife with a broken blade in his pocket. Erickson admitted the weapon belonged to him, and it proved the circumstantial evidence used to convict him. The injured Mattson was conveyed in the patrol wagon to police headquarters. Dr. Horace Davis was urgently called to assist.

During the trial, Dr. Davis was called to testify. His dramatic, nearly sensational presentation captivated everyone in the courtroom. He recounted in detail how he hurriedly made his way to the police station and found an unconscious Mattson, who had blood trickling down the side of his face and a knife blade sticking out of his cranium. After examination, the patient was removed to St. Mary's Hospital, where he lingered for a few days before dying. After Mattson's death, he made a postmortem examination of the body.

Duluth Police Chief Harry Armstrong, ca. 1895. Courtesy of the University of Minnesota Duluth, Kathryn A. Martin Library, Northeast Minnesota Historical Collections.

The prosecuting attorney asked, "Dr. Davis, did you remove the portion of the skull containing the wound?"

The surgeon replied, "Yes, sir."

"Have you got it with you?"

"I have," replied Dr. Davis.

"Please produce it and show it to the jury in order that they may see for themselves what was the extent of the wound."

The *Duluth News Herald* painted the following scene: "The doctor emptied a small package out of an envelope into his left hand and then unrolled the tissue paper covering, stepped down from the stand with the ghastly evidence in his hand and commenced showing it to the jury. At this point the spectators forgot themselves in their interest and witnesses, counsel, court officers, deputies and all present flocked as near to the jury as they dared and stretched their necks to get a glimpse of the blood-stained relic, which showed too plainly where the knife blade had passed through. Even the murderer, Erickson, started forward in his seat and manifested the only interest he has shown since the trial commenced." He was found guilty and charged with manslaughter in the first degree.

Sources: "The Erickson Trial," *Duluth News Herald*, November 22, 1892, 8; and "A Foul Murder," *Duluth Evening Herald*, September 22, 1892, 1.

murder. One witness said Hayward was in Superior in August and lost $500 playing faro, a card game. Another, Edith Weade, whose father owned the Lafayette Hotel in West Superior, recalled a week after Hayward's arrest a memorable episode that took place in August, as well. She believed a woman who may have been Olson and who was accompanied by a young, good-looking gentleman, paid the hotel a visit:

> *Lena and this man came to our hotel and stopped long enough for Lena to do up her hair. I was around and while she was working with her hair, I noticed the bangles on her wrist, the same apparently that were on the Oatka Beach victim. I saw the remains in Duluth ten days after the murder, and while they were in bad state of preservation then I am sure she was the same woman whom I saw at our hotel. The bangles were identical. The couple said something about a preacher before they left the hotel that day and we concluded they were going to get married.*

When Weade was shown a picture of several men unknown to her, she immediately pointed to one and said, "Why that one looks like the man who was here with Lena Olson. ... The way his hair is combed and his mustache curled is exactly like Lena's friend. His face was rather long, at least not fleshy. He was a good looking man who might be anywhere from twenty-eight to thirty-two years of age." The man she pointed to was none other than Hayward. Later, her brother, Fred, was questioned. He, too, followed suit by identifying the same man in the photograph as Hayward.

Although the Weade story was widely circulated in the press, the underlying fact was that without hard evidence connecting Austin and Hayward, pursuing the lead would likely prove fruitless; especially because Hayward did not give up his miserable confederates, including the supposed Austin.

Interestingly, while Hayward sat in jail, his keepers noticed he took a keen interest in the Olson murder case. When asked if he had anything to do with it, he simply replied, "No; that is poppycock."

CHAPTER FIVE
Grasping at Straws

R eaders of the January 20, 1895, issue of the *Duluth News Tribune* were stunned by the bold headlines: "Know His Face. Police at Last Have a Photograph of Lena Olson's Murderer. Very Sure He Is the Man."[14] The events leading up to this discovery began to unfold several weeks earlier when Detective Benson had been informed that the suspect A.A. Austin was possibly living in Chicago.

First, the officer approached the St. Louis County, Minnesota, Commissioners and was given an appropriation of $75 to scour Chicago's vast rogues' gallery of photographed criminals with the intent of identifying the murderer. Lizzie Olson, Lena's younger sister, who in the past five months was described as "indefatigable in her efforts to bring Austin to justice," accompanied Benson to Illinois.

The pair left by the overnight train to the Windy City on Monday evening, January 14. The next morning, they immediately headed to the police headquarters and were ushered into the room containing the mugshot gallery, which featured 26,000 photographs of every kind of crook and cutthroat. "It will take you a month to go through all the pictures in the gallery," a Chicago officer told Benson. "Well, we'll go through as far as we can," he replied.

Over the next two days, the twenty-six-year-old Olson inspected over 12,000 photographs in a thoroughly monotonous, numbing process. She was presented with one image after another. Momentarily gazing at each scoundrel before her, she shook her head and moved on to the next photograph. Benson commented that during their two days of work, Olson hardly spoke a word. Her reserved and taciturn disposition quickly changed on Thursday morning when Benson, who was standing on the opposite side of the room talking to a policeman, heard Olson shriek, "That is him!"[15]

Benson hurried to her side and looked at the photograph held in her trembling hand. "That is Austin! That is Austin!"[16] Olson repeated with conviction.

"Are you sure?" asked Benson, hoping for the world it was true.

"Yes, I am sure," she replied. "I met Austin too often not to know him now. That is him." The devious looking man was named James Driscoll, alias O'Shea, a well-traveled pickpocket about forty-five years old with black hair and blue eyes. He had been arrested in Chicago on December 20, 1892, in the company of known thieves. After serving a light sentence, he was released.

With the identification of Olson's murderer in hand, copies of Driscoll's image were immediately distributed to authorities across the nation. Benson speculated the fiend would be apprehended within two weeks. By Saturday, January 19, Benson and Olson had returned to Minnesota. Their elation in pinpointing Austin was soon and utterly deflated by Minneapolis detective James Doyle, who refuted their certainty regarding Driscoll as

*Joseph Adams alias James Driscoll alias O'Shea alias A.A. Austin. Courtesy of
the Minnesota Historical Society Newspaper Digital Hub.*

Austin. In an interview published by the *Minneapolis Tribune*
on Tuesday, January 22, he said:

> *"It seems to me that I recognize that face," he said, unlocking
> the rogues' gallery. After glancing over the pictures for a few
> minutes his eyes rested upon one, and taking it from the gal-
> lery he said: "Yes, here it is. Joe Lawrence and I arrested this
> man and two other crooks giving the names of John Williams
> and James Walters during the Republican convention [held in
> Minneapolis, June 7–10, 1892]. They were detained during the
> week of the convention on general principles and finally turned
> loose. I remember this man," pointing to the picture labelled
> Joseph Adams, "more distinctly than the rest, because of the*

way he carried his head. Like the average crook, he had a habit of carrying his head down, and raised his eyes when addressed instead of his head."

"This picture," referring again to the picture bearing the name of Joseph Adams, "is one of a dozen taken during the week of the convention, as also is the picture taken [identified] from the Chicago gallery by Detective Benson. It is customary to photograph thieves like these fellows were, and pictures of them, together with the description and crime for which they are arrested, are sent to other cities. We receive others in exchange. The Chicago gallery secured a picture of this man Adams, and the one Benson found there is one of the dozen sent from Minneapolis."

"Admitting that this is the picture of the pickpocket whom you arrested, why is it not possible that this pickpocket and Austin are one and the same person?" was asked of Doyle. "Well, in the first place," was the reply, "pickpockets as a rule don't change their line of work to that of murder. In the second place the description of Austin and that of this man are entirely different."

"It is true that Austin is about forty years of age, and has dark hair. He also wore a heavy brown mustache, the same as this man, but he is a large man, and his face is fuller. When last seen Austin wore short side-burns. He weighs about 170 pounds. He has a square chin, while this man's chin is peaked. The most important distinction between the two men, however, is their talk. Austin has an English accent in his pronunciation of words, and the pickpocket has not."

To prove more conclusively that Benson and Olson were mistaken in the identification, Doyle accompanied the reporter to the home of one of Lena Olson's friends, the dressmaker Thea Larson, who also had known Austin in person. When she answered the door, Doyle handed her the picture of Driscoll, "Do you recognize that face?"

"No," Larson said. Then the detective said the image was believed to be none other than Austin. "No, it is not his picture. It does not resemble him in the least. The mustache is somewhat similar, but the general outline of the features is not the same."

For the remainder of 1895, the Lena Olson murder case nearly fizzled out. The Driscoll affair faded away without further mention. A few incidents, however, sparked interest, even if not quite related to the case. One such scene involved a North Dakotan named Charles Delos, who was arrested for sending obscene materials through the mail, which was a federal offense. Found guilty and insane, he was sentenced to the National Insane Asylum in Washington, DC. En route by train, Delos decoyed his attendants and jumped off in St. Paul. Captured the next day, he was delusional in thinking he had been mistaken for the murderer Austin. Screaming wildly, he declared, "I'm not him! I'm not him!"[17]

From mid-March to mid-May, the name Lena Olson, albeit a different woman, was once again in the headlines: "Killed her child. Betrayed and Abandoned." The twenty-three-year-old domestic servant from St. Paul gave birth to a boy on Sunday, March 17. Within hours of the delivery, fear and shame of her circumstances took over her faculties. Betrayed and deserted by her lover, she placed the newborn at the bottom of her trunk, placed clothes on top of him, and closed the lid. His body was not discovered until the following Thursday. Charged with murder, Olson was acquitted by a jury sympathetic to her circumstances.

Interest in the Lena Olson murder case waned considerably in the second half of 1895. However, the impending execution of Harry Hayward for the murder of Kitty Ging set before sunrise on December 11 kept the story and its possible connection alive. Officials hoped that Hayward would either confess to Olson's murder before he swung from the gallows or give up the perpetrator's identity and whereabouts. Numerous newspapers throughout the land reprinted the statement given the year previous by Hayward's confederate, Claus Blixt, who was serving a life sentence, and who had asserted that Hayward orchestrated Olson's death.

Harry T. Hayward, the day before his execution, December 11, 1895. Courtesy of the Minnesota Historical Society Newspaper Digital Hub.

Hennepin County Deputy Sheriff Gordon Bright sat with Hayward in his final earthly hours. The prisoner enjoyed talking to Bright and opened up to him about many things from his past. As an indiscriminate killer, Hayward boasted that his first killing—a horse—while in St. Louis, was followed by shooting a Black man to death in San Antonio, Texas. There was another shooting episode in Denver, Colorado, but the man lived.

Interrupting, Bright bluntly said, "Harry, you were just a common cruel murderer. Now, why wasn't you as sharp as that fellow who killed the Olson woman? There was a great crime, and the man never was nor never will be discovered. Why couldn't you be as sharp as he was?"

"Well, I'll tell you. There were only two men who knew anything about that Olson murder, and one of them is dead now." Hayward, the proverbial "dead man walking" may very well have been referring to himself as the dead one.

Bright countered, "What do you mean, Harry?"

His last and final words on the subject before his appointment with the hangman's rope were, "Just what I said, that's all."

By February 5, 1896, Duluthians were once again diverted from other sensational and lurid stories in the press, including the murder of an unidentified web-toed woman from Kentucky and the slaying of a family of seven in Chicago. It was at this same time that the most promising lead to date in the Lena Olson case arrived on Chief Armstrong's desk. A letter, postmarked from Little Falls, New York, offered startling information of the whereabouts of Austin.

The unnamed writer had once roomed with a man in Elmira, New York, whom he believed closely matched the alleged murderer's description and history. After living in New York for several years and occasionally using the alias "Adelbert A. Austin," the roommate supposedly traveled out west for a time. However, it was now understood this man was locked up in the county jail at Pomeroy, Ohio, under the name of Albert Johnson.

Armstrong immediately telegraphed the sheriff at Pomeroy, Meigs County, to ascertain whether the description of Austin paired with the man in custody. The following day, a short reply came not to the chief, but to St. Louis County Sheriff William W. Butchart. "I am certain I have A.A. Austin. Will you divide reward? A.P. Ashworth."[18]

Butchart answered that the $500 reward could be divided between the New York informant and Ashworth but insisted on a photograph of the man named Johnson, who was being held at Pomeroy. In the week that followed, the Zenith City police and the local press anxiously waited for the post from the sheriff in Ohio. Headlines included "It is Believed That Lena Olson's Slayer Has Been Found" and "Mystery Solved."

The photograph arrived the evening of Wednesday, February 19. It featured a man about forty years old with a high forehead and a light-colored, drooping mustache. His hair was somewhat thin over the brow. Benson commented, "The picture was by no means the best obtainable. It is only a proof and shows the man dressed as a convict in a calico [dark woolen] shirt and trousers. When Austin was in the Northwest he was always fairly well dressed."

Nevertheless, the picture presented a striking likeness to that of Driscoll, who was identified by Lizzie Olson the year before. Brimming with confidence, Butchart and Benson decided to take the eleven-fifteen p.m. train to Minneapolis that same night and show the photograph to those personally acquainted with Austin. Benson noted, "Sheriff Ashworth of Pomeroy has certainly acted in a very peculiar manner. A couple of pages of description would have aided us wonderfully, but so far all we have been able to get from him is the photograph and assurances that the man is the much-wanted murderer."[19]

Upon arriving in the Twin Cities, the two men proceeded to knock on doors in the early morning hours. Nearly a dozen people, most likely sound asleep, were rudely awakened and shown the photograph forwarded by Ashworth. Lizzie Olson was not among them, as she had moved to South Dakota to live with her brother. The majority concurred the picture was indeed Austin, but to make sure, Thea Larson advised the authorities to bring the fellow back to Minnesota for closer inspection.

Returning to Duluth after seven a.m., Butchart said, "I was so thoroughly satisfied with the result of our visit, that after consulting with Chief Armstrong we concluded to send Detective Benson down to Pomeroy to investigate, and if appearances justify, to bring back the man. Benson did not take extradition papers as I reason if the man is really not Austin he will be perfectly willing to come, while if the identification is correct he will make every effort to escape being brought here."

Without delay, Benson embarked by train for Pomeroy, located in southeast Ohio near the West Virginia border. He arrived Saturday, February 22, at noon. "When I jumped from the train I was met at the station by three officious men who escorted me up to the residence of Sheriff Ashworth." The newly built county jail was styled in gray sandstone featuring two corner towers with curved windows and capped by Peach Bottom roofing slate.

"On the way two more men joined the party, and when we reached the house the sheriff introduced all five as newspaper correspondents. They sat with us in the room while I inquired about the supposed Austin." The sheriff's orchestration of the unveiling of his prized prisoner spoke to his desire to make a big splash.

Meigs County Sheriff's Office and Jail, Pomeroy, Ohio, ca. 1896. Courtesy of Meigs County Sheriff's Office.

At thirty-eight years old, Ashworth had made something of his life from running a hardware store to studying law. Now in his charge was likely the man who for two and half years had baffled lawmen in pursuit. Benson was not interested in small talk but insisted on immediately meeting the suspect. His account of the next hours were detailed in a Duluth newspaper that interviewed him shortly after returning home:

> *"I've got an awfully bad man," said the sheriff, shaking his head to emphasize his words. When he had repeated that sentence two or three times I began to feel that we had a real tough customer to deal with. ... I suggested to the official, who is a young fellow,*

that he bring the man in where I could see him and talk to him in the light. Ashworth demurred and said he felt afraid to bring the suspected man in where he might jump through a window or something and get away. He felt it best not to take chances with a prisoner worth $500. Finally, I overcame his objections, and after I had persuaded the correspondents to withdraw, Johnson, the suspected murderer, was brought in.

Imagine my surprise to find the desperate man, a loutish countrified fellow, who was in no more humor to attempt a break than I was. I turned in and questioned him as if I were sure he was the murderer we were after. He told me his whole story. He was born about forty years ago in New York state, where he lived for several years before he came out west. His name, he said, was Adelbert Johnson, and he worked around on farms until he enlisted in the army in 1884. Then he took the name Albert Austin and served five years, being stationed at Fort Scott [Kansas].

When he was discharged from the army he went to Meigs County, where he has lived ever since. The reason he came to be in jail was because in Ohio obtaining money under false pretenses is a felony. This fellow Johnson started a scheme to turn farm hands into detectives at $10 a head. For this sum he would give a pair of handcuffs, a big tin star, a book with the pictures of a lot of bad men, and a big commission, with a three inch seal.

Johnson picked up two suckers in Meigs County, and was run in for obtaining money under false pretenses. He is awaiting the action of the grand jury. I verified all the statements the fellow made, and when he declared he was perfectly willing to go with me to Minneapolis or anywhere else, I told him I guess we did not want him.

*He is about five feet seven and a half inches in height and weighs
162 pounds, while Austin was over six feet and weighed nearly
200 pounds. If the sheriff had used a little common sense it would
have saved a lot of trouble and expense. Ashworth was perfectly
able to prove the man's statements, but he appears to have gone
off the handle when he thought of the reward. He has not had
very much experience.*

The experience once again proved to be a wild goose chase
of mistaken identity—as a matter of fact, the twentieth such case
since the murder of Lena Olson on August 21, 1894. Benson
wired Chief Armstrong, "This is positively not our man."[20]
In the past two and a half years, the frustrated and exhausted
detective had pursued Austin's trail to twenty different cities,
journeyed thousands of miles over rail, interviewed hundreds
of parties, and followed up on countless clues. The Pomeroy
debacle, which to the authorities was the most significant and
palpable of all cases thus far, quickly vanquished any hope in
bringing Olson's slayer to justice.

As if by a strange coincidence, on February 5, 1896, the same
day Armstrong received the letter from Little Falls, New York,
regarding the suspect Johnson held in Pomeroy, the results of
the previous night's election were announced in the local daily
papers. Henry Truelsen, who believed the police department
was corrupt and singled out Benson in particular, won the
mayorship.

Longtime reporter, editor, and publisher John L. Morrison
recounted many years later the weeks leading up to the election
in his February 9, 1918, publication of the often-bombastic

newspaper *The Duluth Rip-Saw.* Morrison, who had his share of run-ins with Benson in the 1890s, remained resolute in his low opinion of the detective. Morrison described him in his "Tales of the Town" column as a blackmailer who "shook down liquor dealers, red light folk, gamblers and anyone else that came within his reach." Furthermore, he wrote oddly in the third person:

> *Morrison, the reporter, knowing much about the corruption in high places, was one of the Truelsen speakers throughout that campaign. His duty was to tell the voters about the undesirability of Benson and such graft stories as he knew. The people howled their displeasure. At nearly every public meeting, the audience would yell, "How about Bob Benson?" which compelled Truelsen to emphatically say: "Gentlemen, if I am elected mayor of the city of Duluth, I hereby promise that Bob Benson will not be retained in the police department."*

Morrison was recalling the January 21, 1896, election rally when mayoral candidate Truelsen was then quoted as saying, "Who is Bob Benson? He is the man who shot a small boy when we had a strike a few years ago [1889] and then wanted his salary raised as a reward. I promise you there won't be room for both of us when I am elected." After this pronouncement, "there was a prodigious cheer."

The statement that Benson shot "a small boy," is erroneous, and one that was perpetuated for decades, particularly by Morrison in his newspaper. For instance: "Benson ... in a pitched battle, shot a boy. Ever after that, Benson's name was poison at the West End" and "Benson was a very unpopular man in the city, especially in the West End, where he came into special disfavor as the result of shooting a boy in a strike."

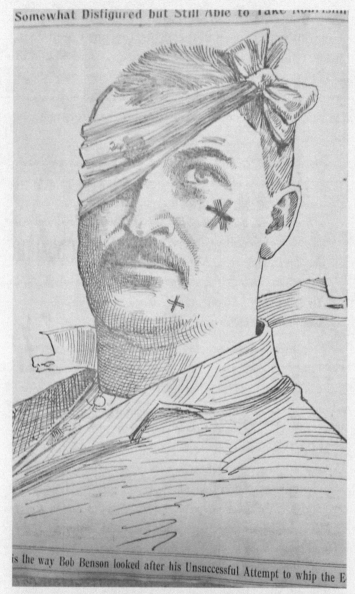

Detective Bob Benson suffers in print at the hands of Duluth Citizen *editor John L. Morrison. Courtesy of the University of Minnesota Duluth, Kathryn A. Martin Library, Northeast Minnesota Historical Collections.*

LAMPOONING DETECTIVE BOB BENSON

The controversial editor and publisher of *The Duluth Rip-Saw*, John L. Morrison (1863–1926), held for decades a great disdain for Detective Bob Benson. Their mutual dislike started not long after Morrison arrived in the port city in 1893 as a reporter for the *Duluth Evening Herald*. Within the next few years, he accused Benson and others in the police department of graft.

The two men finally squared off in a fisticuffs episode that occurred in early June 1896. In his February 9, 1918, issue of the *Rip-Saw*, Morrison fondly recalled the event: "Benson then was well written up and cartooned. The entire community went wild. Copies of the paper went everywhere." What he failed to mention was that the short-lived newspaper, the *Duluth Citizen*, was published by none other than himself. Morrison added, "Many a man who hated Benson got gloriously drunk over the cartoon that showed how Benson looked when he got through trying to whip the editor." The cartoon's top banner read: "Somewhat Disfigured but Still Able to Take Nourishment." The bottom banner read: "This is the way Bob Benson looked after his Unsuccessful Attempt to whip the Editor."

The festering sentiments that Morrison held for Benson were routinely printed in his press between 1917 and 1918. A few choice uncharitable gems included: "The notorious Bob Benson was chief of detectives under Armstrong and everything was fish that came to his nasty net" and the "city detective Benson could not track a load of hay."

Sources: "Desperate Bob Benson Assaults the Editor of The Citizen," *Duluth Citizen*, June 6, 1896, 1; "Tales of the Town," *The Duluth Rip-Saw*, June 23, 1917, 2; July 7, 1917, 2; August 18, 1917, 2; and February 9, 1918, 2.

As mentioned in Chapter 4, Benson reportedly shot and killed striker Edward Johnson, twenty-two.

Another young man, Thomas Fitzsimmons, eighteen, was noted in the *Minneapolis Tribune* (July 11, 1889) as only "an onlooker" or spectator. This was refuted by the *Duluth Evening Herald* (July 8, 1889), which reported, "The boy Fitzsimmons, who was first supposed to be a non-combatant, is said by a well-known man to have fired three shots at the officers. When he was shot [in the abdomen], he threw up his hand, holding the revolver and when he fell the weapon slipped some distance from him." At this point, a man named John Shay, who was also identified as a spectator, apparently picked up Fitzsimmons's gun and tried to carry it away. He was fired upon and one of his fingers was shot off. Fitzsimmons died in the morning on July 8. His remains were taken to Clinton, Ontario, his former home and birthplace.

On February 25, 1896, upon returning from a disappointing trip to Pomeroy, Ohio, Benson surely realized that his days on the force were numbered. Within a short time, Truelsen made good on his campaign promise and fired Benson, Hayden, and Armstrong on March 10. A newspaper quipped, "They will no more follow the trail of the crook and detect stolen stoves in pawn shops." Truelsen appointed his nephew, Iwan Hansen, to replace Armstrong as the new chief.

Benson immediately opened a private detective agency in Duluth, specializing in "high-grade detective work" and aided by "his force of operatives who will assist the veteran sleuth are all first-class." Hayden opened a saloon in town. Armstrong took an extended vacation on the Pacific coast. And without any official pursuers, the Olson murder case was resigned to linger in the shadows.

Oil portrait of Duluth Mayor Henry Truelsen by David Ericson, 1910. Courtesy of the Duluth Public Library, Duluth, Minnesota.

CHAPTER SIX
The Final Clues

Mrs. Elizabeth Guimond long held her suspicions about a particular lodger who first presented himself to her on March 21, 1894. A complete stranger, he sought a room at her Minneapolis boarding house, 313 University Avenue Northeast. "I had been in the habit of taking a few roomers, but was always very careful who they were. On inquiring about him he told me his name was Albert Ellenson, and that he had been boarding at the West Hotel, but preferred a quieter place. I mistrusted him from first sight, but allowed him the use of the room."[21]

Ellenson roomed at Guimond's establishment for five weeks before leaving on April 26, stiffing his landlady for the entire bill. During his short stay, he made a definite impression on her. "He claimed to be in the brokerage business, and frequently won large sums of money, I soon found that he was not as well fixed as he said." Yet, he put on airs, telling Guimond about his interests in such things as grand English estates.

The peculiar boarder also requested that she give him any letters that arrived addressed to a "Mr. A.A. Austin." It struck her as odd, and she asked him to explain why he went by two names. Ellenson replied it was simply a matter of business convenience. He used the name Austin when registering at hotels.

By all appearances, Ellenson was down on his luck. He frequently asked her for money to invest in wheat speculation, which she always declined. "One day he asked me for $10, which I refused him. He pleaded with tears in his eyes, and as a last resort volunteered to put up his valise, which he claimed contained a number of valuable articles. I gave him $10." He soon disappeared without leaving a forwarding address.

Later in the spring, Guimond and her husband were walking on Nicollet Avenue when they happened upon Ellenson and a companion. She wasted little time in demanding her money. Anxious to extricate himself from the confrontation, Ellenson told Guimond he was in a hurry but promised to call at her house soon to settle the matter. "I thought I would get a look at his friend, and did. The man had a peculiar set of teeth."

Months passed, and Ellenson's empty promise of repayment festered within Guimond. She decided to

West Hotel, Minneapolis, Minnesota, ca. 1880–1910. Meeting place for A.A. Austin and Lena Olson. Courtesy of the Hennepin County Library, James K. Hosmer Special Collections Library.

James E. Alsop alias Albert A. Austin alias Albert Ellenson, suspected murderer of Lena Olson. Courtesy of the Minnesota Historical Society Newspaper Digital Hub.

open the battered, leather valise that he had left as collateral. Within it she found revealing papers and letters addressed to a man named James E. Alsop from Tacoma, Washington. Alsop was by no means a stranger to Minneapolis as Guimond soon learned. Several clippings attested to his arrest for real estate fraud in December 1892.

Not long after opening the bag, Guimond by chance met Ellenson again in August 1894 visiting Minnehaha Falls on a Sunday afternoon. This time he was in the company of a young woman, showing her the sights. "I stopped him and

Stereoview of Minnehaha Falls, Minneapolis, Minnesota, 1897. Courtesy of the Hennepin County Library, James K. Hosmer Special Collections Library.

told him that I knew everything about him, and unless he gave me the money I would have him arrested. He said, 'Come on Miss Olson.' I remember the words distinctly," she said. The following day, Ellenson sent the $10 he had borrowed from her but failed to arrange picking up his old valise. She never saw him again after their encounter at the picturesque falls.

In late January 1895, Guimond, like many others, was fascinated with the Harry T. Hayward case. Facing first-degree murder, his trial was an enticing draw for her. Sitting in the gallery, she immediately identified Hayward, with his horsey teeth, as the same person encountered with Ellenson on Nicollet Avenue the previous spring. Furthermore, the published insinuations that a connection existed between A.A. Austin, the alleged murderer of Lena Olson, and Hayward made sense to her particularly because Ellenson asked that he be given any mail that arrived addressed to Albert Austin.

Plus, while boarding with her, she understood he frequented the Ozark Flats where Hayward resided. Even the description of the mysterious Austin tallied perfectly to that of her lodger Ellenson, she thought.

Without delay, she sent a letter to the Minneapolis police, asking for a detective to be sent to her house. Unfortunately, no officer was dispatched. Later on, a newspaper chastised her, "Womanlike, she forgot the [to include her] address and the request could not be granted." And for whatever reason, Guimond did not follow up on her startling revelation for another year. After Detective Benson's last foray to Pomeroy, Ohio, in February 1896, and with the Olson murder case noticeably winding down in later March, she decided to contact the authorities one final time.

Detective John J. Courtney, a nine-year veteran of Minneapolis' finest, called at Guimond's house within days of receiving her second post. He inspected the contents of the valise and concluded that the clues found were indeed promising. There was a yellowed clipping from November 1890 telling of a Mrs. Mary Alsop's tragic death, which resulted from a runaway carriage accident. A will was made and signed by her husband, James E. Alsop, prior to her death. In it, he bequeathed to her all his property with the exception of a dollar to each of his sons. Interestingly, the will at some point was later marked "cancelled."

Courtney found it rather strange that Alsop had kept the cancelled will but noted, "I think the fellow probably aided in her death, and in case any question ever arose, he intended to produce that document to show how much he had thought of her." The bag also contained a fine silk handkerchief, which the police later identified as having belonged to none other than the notorious Harry Hayward.

With the bona fide signature of Alsop, alias Ellenson, the police engaged a handwriting expert to compare the will against the signature "A.A. Austin and wife," penned in Duluth's Merchant's Hotel register on August 21, 1894. Without a doubt, the scrawl in the former mimicked exactly the register's entry; the penmanship was deemed "a trifle crude and peculiar" by the expert. Most noticeable handwriting characteristics found in each document were the peculiar crossing of the *t*'s, and the dotting of the *i*'s.

Armed with credible evidence, Minneapolis police chief Smith secretly instructed Courtney to head to the West Coast on April 7, 1896, and track down Alsop, alias Austin, alias Ellenson. Why Smith did not send along one of the two officers, Hoy and McNulty, who arrested Alsop and charged him with fraud on December 11, 1892, is a mystery. The men certainly could have properly identified him. As a favor to the investigation, the Great Northern Railroad furnished free transportation to Courtney, who was on the chase of his life, hunting down a fugitive killer ripe for the rope.

The one constant description given of James E. Alsop was that he fancied himself a well-heeled Englishman. He was born in the spring of 1846, most likely in late April. The exact location of his birth is uncertain, but it was probably in the Midlands.[22] In July 1848, parents thirty-year-old John and twenty-six-year-old Mary Ann decided to take their four young sons (William, six; Thomas, four; James, two; and infant Charles) and immigrate to America.

In London, the family along with 171 passengers boarded the 971-ton brig *Delta* bound for New York City. After 40 days of sailing across the Atlantic Ocean, the Alsops arrived on August 24. The family settled and farmed in the Butternuts-Gilbertsville area, Otsego County, New York.

When war sounded between the states in April 1861, the eldest son William, nineteen, answered the call. He enlisted in the fall of 1861 for three years with Company E, New York 2nd Heavy Artillery. After engaging in major battles that included Bull Run, the Second Battle of Bull Run, Cedar Creek, and Spotsylvania, Private Alsop was wounded in the left foot on May 31, 1864, at Totopotomoy Creek, Virginia. He mustered out in October 1864.

William, older brother of James E. Alsop. Courtesy of The Gilbertsville Free Library, Gilbertsville, New York.

Commercial Street, Gilbertsville, New York, ca. 1890. The village was the childhood home of James E. Alsop. Courtesy of The Gilbertsville Free Library, Gilbertsville, New York.

In the years that followed, William suffered from his crippling war injury, but "bore the affliction without a murmur." In 1886, he passed away at the age of forty-four. His death was attributed to lead poisoning or "painters' colic" as it was known then, a common complaint in his occupation as a painter. His obituary stated he was respected by those who knew him and a good citizen.

The second son, Thomas, at age nineteen, enlisted for three years in August 1863 with Company K, New York 64th Infantry Regiment. He was killed at the battle of Nye River, Virginia, on May 15, 1864.

There is no reference to support that the third son, James, served at all while the war raged and finally concluded after four devastating years in April 1865. However, a fourteen-year-old "James Allsop" enlisted in New York City in August 1861, as a musician with the Third Regiment, Irish Volunteers, Company B. There is, however, a possibility that this young man may have been none other than James E. Alsop (as determined by state census records and spelling variations of the surname). Whether Allsop was a drummer boy or a bugler is unknown, but according to military records, James Allsop deserted on January 26, 1863, from camp near Falmouth, Virginia.

On January 1, 1867, James Alsop married Mary J. Hollis of Gilbertsville. By 1880 they had three children: John, twelve; George, eleven; and Katherine, two.[23] In November of that same year, James' father, John, passed away. The following spring, James' brothers Charles (who went by his middle name of John) and Adelbert, born 1857, ventured to Kansas.[24] James followed suit in the spring of 1883. In a February 15, 1884, letter from Norton, Kansas, to the Gilbertsville *Otsego Journal*, James Alsop apprised readers of his doings in the past year:

> *Through your columns I wish to give my impressions of Kansas, having now been a resident of the state for the past year. Until recently I have been residing in Waterville, which is comparatively in the eastern part of the state. The country there can no longer be called new. For it has all the advantages of an old settled country. Fine, well cultivated farms, nice young orchards, good houses and barns, fine churches and schools; all these are of common occurrence. It is a splendid farming country, but lands are high and no such openings exist as can be found in a new country.*

From the post-mark of this you will see that I write from north western Kansas. I came here but a few days since, and I am so well pleased with the country that I have concluded to make it my future home. I find some of the pioneers of this new country are former Otsego boys, and they are all satisfied with their location.

... I am told that this country presents a very different appearance from what it did at the time of its settlement, only a few years since; then it was a vast hunting ground, when countless herds of buffalo fed upon the rich native grasses. Now the country numbers not less than 6,000 in population. A railroad penetrates the southern part of the county. About eighty-five school districts are organized, newspapers are published through the county, churches are established, three of them in Norton—Methodist, Presbyterian and Christian. New towns are springing up. Six flouring mills are in operation and business of all kinds common to a new country is to be found flourishing here. I find this country has been badly misrepresented by many who have given it an imperfect trial and then left.

... Norton is a thriving town and running over with business. I believe more business is done here in one day than is done in Gilbertsville in two weeks, and yet the town is no larger than Gilbertsville. It contains four general stores, two hardware, two millinery, and the usual amount of hotels, shops etc., generally found in a thriving place.

... Society is excellent, health is good and the climate is certainly delightful. Taking everything in consideration, I am highly pleased with the county and the people, and I can see no reason why this country may not, in a few years, take rank with the populous and wealthy counties on the eastern part of the state,

Respectfully, J.E. Alsop

Norton, Kansas, held promise as the land of milk and honey. Alsop secured a couple of farms, and in cooperation with one of his wife's relatives, the Hollises, was lent tools and stock. According to newspaper reports, Alsop raised some good crops and improved the farms. By January 1885, the fledgling community of Norton was suffering a bust and no one was making money.

Adding to his troubles, Alsop was later implicated in a lawsuit over property rights. The case, *Solomon M. Hollis, et. al., v. Isaac W. Burgess* was adjudicated by the Kansas State Supreme Court. During the same year, Alsop and family relocated sixty miles south, settling in WaKeeney, Trego County, that spring. The same year, Alsop's mother, Mary, joined them.

As a sheep farmer two miles east of town, he suffered near ruin in the harsh winters of 1885 and 1886, losing nearly everything. Undaunted, he persevered wearing a variety of hats in the community the following two years. In the summer of 1886, he was appointed under sheriff and marshal. Hardly a week passed where his name was not mentioned in the local newspaper, including descriptions like "well known" and "our excellent friend."

Alsop dabbled in real estate, developed lots in town, served as city canvasser, was selected as a delegate for the state Republican convention, and was recognized as a pillar in the local Methodist church. His honesty was noted when he found a silk handkerchief left on a pew, and then advertised in the newspaper for the owner to reclaim it.

As a public authority, his exploits made for good reading. For instance, the following was printed in the local newspaper in March 1887: "A couple of women bearing a rather unenviable reputation located themselves temporarily on the outskirts of

East Side, WaKeeney, Kansas, 1885. The village was home to the James E. Alsop family for several years during the mid-1880s. Courtesy of the Trego County Historical Society, WaKeeney, Kansas.

town last week. City Marshal Alsop waited upon them and ordered them to pack up and leave, which they did."

A few months later, a story titled "Boys on a Bum," detailed the adventures of three youths, ages ranging from ten to twelve. Two of the boys were sons of the sheriff from neighboring Ellis County, and the other boy was the son of the Ellis County attorney. According to the clipping, the boys were mounted, armed, and dressed. "They were bent for 'way out west."[25] When arriving in WaKeeney, Marshal Alsop suggested they stay overnight and rest before heading farther into the great wide wilderness. In the meantime, he telegraphed the parents who arrived the next day by train to retrieve their sons.

In late August 1887, Alsop announced his candidacy for county sheriff. The newspaper editor wrote, "He brings to the discharge of his official duties a thorough earnestness, and, in the event of his succeeding in his aspirations, the county would have a creditable sheriff." Two weeks later, Alsop surprised his friends and supporters by withdrawing from the race. Evidently, his health had been poor since early summer. In the months that followed, Alsop resigned his post as city marshal, sold his property, and in November 1887 moved to Tacoma, Washington Territory, where he hoped to improve his condition.

CHAPTER SEVEN
Descent into Ruin

~~~~~~~~~~

The City of Destiny, Tacoma's nickname, would forever hold a lasting, dark meaning for the Alsop family. The boom times of Washington Territory offered great wealth to those who were motivated to seize it, whether by honesty or not. The arrival of the Northern Pacific Railroad in 1873 brought with it immigrants by the thousands in the following decades.

Like Alsop, those who understood development and real estate could prosper. In March 1888, he and fellow WaKeeney transplant William Burroughs formed the firm Burroughs & Alsop. Business was lucrative for the two.

Wanting to appear prosperous, Alsop moved his family to 705 Yakima Avenue, the street of high society. In October 1889 he formed a partnership with several other men with a capital stock of $100,000 (equivalent to $2,842,000 in 2021). They founded the Lake Park Land, Railway & Improvement Company; Alsop was appointed superintendent of the road, Burroughs made vice-president.

The company acquired and sold timber, mineral, and agricultural lands. One of its paramount projects was the

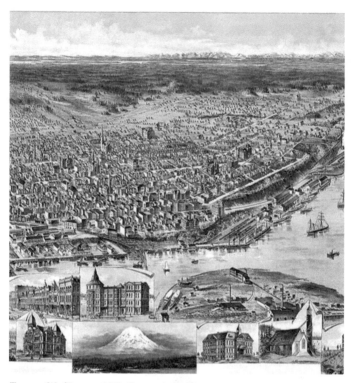

Tacoma, Washington, 1890. Courtesy of author.

undertaking of a planned resort community called Lake Park. Situated on the eastern shores of Spanaway Lake, it was a twenty-minute commute from Tacoma on a "first-class electric street railway."[26] Within a year, allegations of fraud swirled around the railway and its superintendent. Assertions were made that contracts for lots in Lake Park had been altered from the original agreements. Embroiled in financial improprieties, Alsop's misery would come to a head on November 24, 1890.

Early that afternoon, he and his wife Mary borrowed a horse and buggy from Burroughs. Their intent was to visit a house perched on a hill. They had rented the dwelling a few days earlier because an oil lamp had exploded at their home.

Exterior view of the Lake Park Hotel, with a Lake Park Land, Railway &
Improvement Company train in front, Spanaway, Washington, ca. 1895. The
hotel, along with at least two other buildings, burned in 1904. Courtesy of the
University of Washington, Seattle (UW) Libraries, Special Collections Division.

Although the damage was minimal, they immediately arranged
to change their residence. The goal for the afternoon was to
measure the floors of several rooms for carpeting. Finishing
at dusk, they started for home on Yakima Avenue.

According to Alsop, the road was not graded in some places
and was very rough and steep. "We had not gone far when a
part of the harness gave way, and I got out to fix it, handing the
lines to Mrs. Alsop as I did so. As I got down from the buggy
the animal started, then stopped, and the buggy ran against

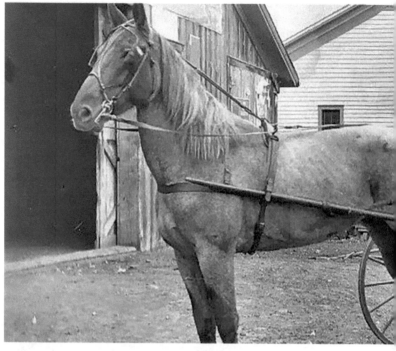

Typical horse and buggy rig, ca. 1890s. Courtesy of author.

him." This frightened the horse, and at once he started down the hill. With no time to react, Alsop said, "It was too late for me to reach his head so I grabbed a hind wheel and tried to stop him in that way. But I was thrown headlong. By the time I could regain my feet the buggy had almost disappeared in the darkness down the narrow, crooked road."

As it was racing down the hill, forty-seven-year-old Mary could not control the buggy. Ahead of her a wagon was coming up the road loaded with hay. Alsop witnessed the collision and said, "As the buggy top was partly up, I couldn't tell whether or not my wife had a hold of the lines. At any rate, the horse and buggy went over into a deep gully with a crash."

Alsop raced down the embankment to Mary's side. "I found my wife lying bruised and insensible in a heap under the ruins of the buggy," said a prostrated husband.[27] Her skull was crushed from hitting a small stump. The horse freed himself from the wreck and disappeared. Alerted by Alsop's cries for help, the driver of the hay wagon and other passersby carried the unconscious Mary to a nearby farmhouse. A doctor was hastily summoned, but despite all efforts, she soon passed away.

Mary was described as "in many particulars a remarkable woman. She was shrinking, sensitive and timid, and yet when set for a principle she was as firm as the mountains. She dreaded publicity, and loved to do her work in a quiet, unostentatious manner. She loved to look after those whom others were likely to neglect," and "She made many friends who had learned to love her for her kindness of heart and true worth."

Following her tragic death and subsequent funeral, Alsop apparently failed to personally notify his wife's relatives in the east. Later, one of her brothers came to Tacoma and requested the body be exhumed, alleging foul play. Alsop, well-connected and influential, had his brother-in-law "hushed up" as it was later reported. Yet, the matter of Mary's death was cause for considerable talk in Tacoma parlors. Mariette Burroughs, the wife of Alsop's business partner, stated years later that she was in possession of an affidavit written by Mary Alsop declaring that her husband had on two occasions tried to poison her.

The first attempt occurred before they moved to Washington. Mary believed he had administered the highly toxic, green crystalline power, Paris green, used as rodenticide and insecticide, in a lettuce salad for her. Suspecting he was up to no good, she declined the dish and then secretly had its contents analyzed. The results, she claimed, showed that enough poison was found in the lettuce to kill three women. Mrs. Burroughs was of the opinion that it was common knowledge among their friends that Mary had lived a most unhappy life with her husband and had met with foul play rather than accidental death.

Another informant, a former neighbor of the Alsops, also confided to the press several years later after Mary's tragic demise:

> She was a most estimable lady, and one whom I had known for years. It was a notorious fact among her immediate neighbors that she was constantly in fear of her husband. I recall one incident in particular well illustrating this. A slick book agent came around in the neighborhood and got a number of ladies,

Mrs. Alsop among the number, to sign a contract to buy a set of books at five cents per week. When the ladies found out what they had signed some time afterwards it was a note for $36 each. The book agent had deposited the notes in the bank. Mrs. Alsop came to our house and discussed the matter with my wife when it became known that the ladies had signed notes instead of contracts.

She was so afraid of Alsop and what he would say about the affair that she was almost crazy. Alsop was a member of my church, but nevertheless I thought him a rascal. His very looks showed it. When he married his first wife [Mary] she had considerable property. He got possession of it all, however. Alsop personally was always in some kind of a swindling deal. He had rather make $500 by cheating someone than make it honestly. At one time he purchased some land from a Tacoma barber and sold it to other parties for so much down and the balance on time. They paid the money down and when they went to make the second payment found that Alsop had arranged matters so that their equity in the property expired some time previous.[28]

In the years immediately following his wife's death, Alsop sold his share of the railway for $25,000 (equivalent to $719,000 in 2021) and moved to the newly established community of Lake Park. By all appearances he was a devoted father to his only child living at home, Kate, who turned fourteen in 1892. Perhaps seeking a mother for her, Alsop courted a restaurant cashier and recent divorcée, thirty-three-year-old Julia Ann Minthorn (née Dodge) and married her on September 7, 1892.

For their extended honeymoon or "bridal tour," as it was then called, Alsop boasted of returning to his birthplace, England, and possibly touring Europe. The first stop of their journey was to visit Minnesota where his new wife's relatives resided. His in-laws were stunned to learn the man she introduced as her husband was not Fred Minthorn, whom she married in 1878, but rather James Alsop. She had not told anyone of her divorce from Minthorn.

Citing a cholera scare in Europe, Alsop decided to forgo traveling abroad. He and Julia settled in for six weeks at the home of her younger sister, Harriet, who lived in Duluth. Harriet's husband, Alphonso R. Walker, a real estate dealer, offered Alsop the use of his office. At one point, Alsop asked Walker to endorse a note for $500 (credit extended to the first party with the endorsing party assuming responsibility for the loan if repayment was not met).

Walker's colleagues did not hold a good impression of Alsop and tried to dissuade him from endorsing the note. To settle the matter, Walker contacted a bank in Tacoma to verify Alsop's financial condition. To his surprise, he was informed that Alsop was worth in excess of $80,000. Soon after the note was granted, the Alsops left for Minneapolis at the end of October.

While in the Flour City, as Minneapolis was also known, Alsop made the acquaintance of Byron T. Randall, one of Walker's former business partners. Like in Duluth, Alsop made himself comfortable in Randall's office located on First Avenue South. He wrote letters and conducted personal business. The Englishman, always stylishly dressed, topped by a silk hat, gave the appearance of a man of wealth and refinement.

Randall said later that he never liked the man, and "set him down for a crook the minute he saw him." In addition, he also understood the $500 note endorsed by Walker was later cashed by Alsop. When it came due, Alsop was nowhere to be found, making Walker liable for reimbursement.

In mid-December 1892, Alsop's shady dealings finally caught up to him. Accused by a former Tacoma associate, George Hollidge, of a sizable land fraud deal amounting to nearly $8,000, Alsop was arrested in Minneapolis. Newspapers declared him to be a first-class swindler. Bailed out of jail by the unsuspecting Walker, the case was soon dismissed by the grand jury as the plaintiff failed to substantiate his case. However, Alsop's name and reputation were besmirched in newspapers across the Northwest. The honeymoon was over.

Returning to Tacoma, the ensuing year of 1893 unfolded for Alsop as a descent into eventual ruin. Unable to make a living selling real estate, he speculated on the market, often losing vast sums. Chicago's stock exchange beckoned Alsop to recoup his losses.

A former roommate, who wished to remain anonymous in print, recounted his association with Alsop when the two boarded together on Michigan Avenue. In a *Minneapolis Tribune* interview, which was published after Alsop's identity became known as the alleged murderer, Anonymous revealed the inner workings of Alsop—a womanizer, a schemer, and a gambler—a man bereft of morals and responsibility.

"I roomed at that place [for] nearly two months, and during that time got quite well acquainted with him. He dressed well, wore a silk hat and curled his mustache every morning with a curler heated in a gas jet. He often spoke of the nice time he had had the evening before with some ladies," said Anonymous.

Alsop spoke to him of fancy suppers and endless wine, playing cards and making money on the stock exchange—often using large sums of money given to him by his new female companions. He admitted to Anonymous that he did not always turn a profit from speculation but greatly enjoyed the thrill of scoring big, even on a few dollars. Alsop also bragged that he had been a success as a real estate businessman in Tacoma and was respected from coast to coast.

Stereoview of Nicollet Avenue, Minneapolis, Minnesota, ca. 1890. Courtesy of the Hennepin County Library, James K. Hosmer Special Collections Library.

Anonymous added that Alsop often spoke affectionately of his wife in Tacoma and showed him a picture of her. "He told me of the nice letters he would receive from her from time to time. He said he left Tacoma without an hour's preparation; was downtown one day and took a sudden notion to come to Chicago and left that day at noon with only a small hand satchel containing a clean shirt and a few other things, which he claimed was the reason for his wearing a light shirt in November and December."

Anonymous judged him to be scraping by, trying to capture a dream without success. "I saw no more of him until in July '94, I met him one evening on Nicollet Avenue [in Minneapolis]. He invited me to call and see him at his rooms, which I did the following Sunday. Up to that time I thought him a nice, gentlemanly fellow, but a little hard up." The following month, Alsop asked to borrow $10 for a pressing bill and promised to repay him as soon as funds arrived from his Tacoma bank. "I didn't hardly believe his story and mistrusted that it was a fraud, and that he was trying to 'work me,' so declined to make the advance. From that time I never saw or heard of him again."

The telling line in the preceding account was the hasty departure of Alsop from Tacoma and arrival in chilly Chicago in November 1893 with literally only the shirt on his back and a spare in his satchel. Perhaps what precipitated his urgency to leave town quickly was undoubtedly tied to deadly events that transpired in the preceding months.

In the cloak of darkness on September 4, 1893, a feeble eighty-year-old named Charlotte Fetting was brutally assaulted. The method of her demise was later found eerily similar in manner to that of Lena Olson, who was murdered the following summer. In each case, the motive behind the crime was money, and without doubt Alsop's nefarious hand was evident.

The elderly Fetting lived with her son, Ernest, in a miserable, rough board shack on the outskirts of south Seattle known as the shantytown district. Their little home was near the crossing of the broad gauge and narrow-gauge tracks. It was said of her, "Mrs. Fetting was an old woman but she loved gold."

Earlier in the summer, fearful of a bank failure, Fetting and her son withdrew $800 in the form of gold, double-eagle coins. They hid the trove in a trunk and kept the secret to themselves. Or so they maintained. Several days leading up to her death, they were visited daily by her son-in-law James King, described as a good-looking Irishman in his early forties from Tacoma. King, recently widowed with four children, worked at a coffin factory. Reportedly, one of his bosom friends was none other than Alsop.

Meeting at a Tacoma saloon on a regular basis, King, Alsop, and a man named William A. Wilcox, an intimate friend of King's, played cards, gambled, and apparently schemed to steal Fetting's gold. On the night she died, her son and King left for the People's Standard Theater around seven o'clock. The entertainment establishment, known for vaudeville acts, was also a well-known haven for two-bit gangsters and ne'er-do-wells who gambled in the basement.

Around ten thirty p.m., a man stealthily made his way along a steep, narrow trail to Fetting's cabin. A half-block away, passenger and coal trains rumbled by every six to ten minutes, drowning out any possible cries for help. The assassin quietly knocked on her door. When she answered, he grabbed her and tried to wrap a flour sack towel around her gray-haired head and subdue her with a bottle of chloroform. Miraculously, the aged woman escaped his clutches momentarily. The intruder caught her again and shoved a large cotton handkerchief in her mouth, gagging her from making any noise. As a final act, her skull was crushed with the stove lid. Soon the fiend located the hidden gold and disappeared.

King and Fetting left the theater after midnight and arrived home around one a.m., finding the door unlocked and partly opened. Fetting immediately exclaimed, "I have been robbed!" Unsure if the burglar was still inside, the two men went next door and woke up the neighbor, seeking assistance. When the men returned with a lantern, they were confronted with a grim sight.

Deemed one of the most horrendous murders in the history of Seattle at that time, the sensational case filled newspapers for weeks to come. Police long suspected King was an accomplice to the murder. He was the one who suggested that his brother-in-law join him at the People's Standard on the night of the crime.

By early November, without a conviction, authorities pressed King to come clean and admit that he conspired with others and that the intended robbery of the aged Fetting went terribly wrong. Rumors on the street were that he never received his share of the booty stolen the night of the murder and was about to turn state's evidence against his dastardly colleagues in crime, possibly including Alsop.

In an act that shocked Tacoma citizens, King was waylaid in the late hours on November 17. A man approached him from behind, withdrew a .38 caliber revolver and fired three shots. The one that struck him behind the left ear killed him instantly, silencing his testimony forever. The next morning, his body was found floating in the shallow waters of Commencement Bay. His coat was buttoned and his pockets unrifled. The police viewed this as a case of intended murder, not robbery. The heat was on to find the culprit or culprits. Within days, William Wilcox, the suspected accomplice, was arrested in Tacoma and charged with the murder of Charlotte Fetting.[29]

At this same time, Alsop told his wife he urgently needed to go to Chicago on business. While away, she claimed he wrote affectionate letters to her. The last word she ever heard from him was that he planned to visit northern Minnesota. She came to believe the reason he did not write to her anymore was that he had perished in the great Hinckley, Minnesota, fire in early September 1894. For the next year and a half, she tried to collect evidence of Alsop's death in order to obtain his life insurance. Little did she know that Minneapolis Detective John Courtney was also trying to track him down once and for all to bring him to justice.

CHAPTER EIGHT
The Murder Avenged

"Hello, Alsop. How are you today?" inquired Detective Courtney, as he approached the tall, slender gentleman from behind. Dressed in a knee-length frock coat and silk hat, Alsop, who had been patiently waiting to collect his mail, turned after Courtney tapped him on the arm. The smiling officer then jovially said, "Why, I used to know you in Tacoma."[30]

"Why, I'm first rate, thank you," he replied without hesitation.

Courtney noticed though that Alsop eyed him quizzically. "I guess you don't know me," continued the detective.

"Say, where is your old partner, Burroughs?"

Alsop answered amiably, "Oh, I think he's broke, like the rest of us."

With acknowledgment of his name and Burroughs, Courtney dropped the pretense of politeness, placed a firm hand on the scoundrel's shoulder, and informed him he was under arrest.

Seattle city hall and police headquarters, 3rd Avenue, south of Jefferson Street, ca. 1896. Courtesy of the University of Washington, Seattle (UW), Libraries, Special Collections Division.

"Why, what's this for? I've done nothing," he said. Courtney observed that Alsop strained to conceal his agitation, but the pallor of his face betrayed him.

"Well, we will see about that later," replied the detective. Joined by Gilman Philbrick, a seasoned Seattle lawman, the two men escorted Alsop over to the police station, where he was booked for murder late on the afternoon of April 16, 1896—exactly 604 days since the slaying of Lena Olson in Duluth.

Following the arrest, the public was stunned by the immediate success of the thirty-five-year-old Courtney in tracking down his man only nine days after departing Minneapolis on

April 7. Newspapers nationwide trumpeted his shrewdness and hailed him as a sleuth extraordinaire.

At the same time, another story developed in Duluth. A distraught woman named Mrs. Gunhilda Peterson, who had agitated officials for some time, claimed that a local plumber had killed both Lena Olson and A.A. Austin, dumping his body in Lake Superior.

She substantiated her statement with several interesting observations. At the time of the Olson murder, Peterson was employed by the plumber. A few days after Olson's body was found, the plumber asked her to wash a bloody shirt and a flour sack. Within a short time, the man left for Michigan. He returned with loads of money and two new trunks filled with recently purchased clothes. According to her, the family was poor, and they were suddenly flush with cash.

The accused plumber thought Peterson was unstable and asked the probate court to examine her. On the afternoon of April 13, Peterson saw her husband sitting in the probate office. She said he should go home, "as his head was too small." The court found her insane and ordered her to the state hospital in Fergus Falls. Sticking to her story, Peterson regretted not seeing the governor in person, whom she thought would follow up on her claim and prosecute the man.

The apprehension of Alsop, and how it unfolded, riveted the nation. The events leading to Alsop's arrest began when Courtney arrived in Seattle. Under the guise of a real estate dealer, he visited the offices of William Burroughs, Alsop's former business partner, on Friday, April 10. Courtney claimed that he carried in his pocket an abstract of a deed for a property that belonged to Alsop and wished to obtain his signature for its transfer. "Why, the man you wish to see was here today," said Burroughs, "and I think he went from here to Tacoma."

The next day, the detective called upon Alsop's second wife, Julia Alsop, and sixteen-year-old daughter Kate. Courtney learned that on April 7, the same day the officer left Minneapolis, Alsop startled his family by appearing at their residence; he had been absent since November 1893. For two hours he entreated his wife to take him back. She was unmoved and showed him the door.

Later that afternoon, she took steps to file for divorce, alleging desertion. Mrs. Alsop told Courtney that her husband had urged his daughter to write to him at the Seattle general delivery post office, where he was receiving letters. With this information, the detective knew he was hot on the trail and it was only a matter of time.

In the following days, he worked closely with Seattle Chief of Police Bolton Rogers. Philbrick was instructed to give his Minneapolis colleague all the assistance within his power. "Stay with him," said Rogers, "until you get the man." Rogers then opened up his book in which descriptions of criminals were kept and withdrew the circular of A.A. Austin, which matched the description in Courtney's possession. Soon, the fugitive would be brought into the clutches of the law.

Courtney and Philbrick devised a plan to stake out the post office. The elderly clerk, who handled the general delivery window, agreed to signal the lawmen when Alsop appeared. The operation commenced on April 16. Courtney said, "I got up bright and early Thursday morning, and went to the post office at seven o'clock. It did not open until one hour later, but I thought it wise to be on deck early." He and Philbrick whiled away the morning and early afternoon loitering about the lobby without success.

Courtney later recounted for the *Minneapolis Tribune* what transpired around two thirty p.m.:

At that time the man I was looking for appeared in the doorway. I knew him the minute I saw him. The circular gave the best description of him that I ever knew of. He would be recognized instantly wherever he was. I was reading a paper, and when he stepped up to the window I slowly walked up behind him. It was an exciting moment in one way, but I have to laugh when I think of an incident that occurred.

The man at the window had agreed to tap lightly on the glass if he thought I did not know Alsop when he entered. He did not think I knew him, although I was standing at his back listening to what was said. The elderly man kept tapping and tapping and fumbling ever the letters, saying he thought there was a letter there for a man of that name, but he did not know where it had been placed. Finally I touched Alsop lightly on the arm.[31]

Once his arrest was made public, the *Duluth News Tribune* lightheartedly opined, "It would indeed be funny if Austin, the murderer of Lena Olson, should be found at Seattle. And yet, why not? The police have looked in every part of the country except Seattle."

While Alsop no doubt understood he was in a tight pickle, he played it cool as he walked up to the police station's registration window. "What is your name?" asked the clerk.

"James E. Alsop," was given in a quick and decisive manner. "How old?"

"Forty-nine," Alsop replied. "I was born in England," he continued. "I think I am five feet eleven inches tall. Oh, I weigh about 175 pounds."

Completing his description profile, his eyes were recorded as brown, hair black. His profession was noted as a real estate dealer. Emptying his pockets, he revealed his worldly wealth amounted to the sum of a single nickel. Alsop was formally charged with the double murders of Lena Olson in August 1894 and Charlotte Fetting in September 1893. Authorities also suspected he most likely killed his first wife in November 1890 and James King in November 1893. The press wasted little time in labeling him "one of the worst criminals of the century."

Courtney thought Alsop concealed the disgrace of his arrest and subsequent charges well and went to his cell with a "stiff upper lip." He was quartered in the empty women's department, away from other wrongdoers held in custody. His sparse and private cell held a plank bunk and a gray blanket.

The detective wasted little time sending a telegram to the proper authorities in Minnesota. He instructed them to arrange all the necessary paperwork for Alsop's immediate extradition. Philbrick, who had learned that the prisoner had lodged at the Queen City Hotel in town, returned after searching his room. He had discovered a large valise containing some revealing contents. In it was a piece of paper, apparently written in Chicago, that purported to be a promissory note for $200. Two names appeared on this document—A. Austin and James Alsop.

Rifling through a trunk also found in Alsop's room, Philbrick uncovered a little memorandum book with corroborating details. Written in the cutthroat's hand, it provided his movements in Minnesota during the spring and summer of 1894. The book also included numerous addresses of women. At the time of Olson's murder on August 21, Alsop noted that he was rooming at a Mrs. Hanna's until Tuesday, August 28, "left Mrs. Hanna owing $49.50." The next day's entry showed he had left the state: "In St. Louis."

Philbrick also learned that the near-penniless Alsop deposited with the hotel landlord pictures of Salt Lake City and Brigham Young as a guarantee of payment for his room, which cost no more than fifty cents a night. In time, the Utah connection would become evident.

The following day, Friday, April 17, Philbrick and Courtney interrogated Alsop and recorded his responses for an affidavit. "Why did you give the name of A.A. Austin in Duluth?" questioned the detective.[32]

"I will tell you," replied Alsop. "I went to Chicago with somewhere in the neighborhood of $2,000 and bucked the stock market and lost it all. I went broke and went to Duluth. I have been in Duluth when I was well fixed and so did not want people that knew me to know where I was. When a man's broke and has to live on two bit meals, sleep in two bit beds and has seen better days he don't care to have friends know it. That was my reason." The prisoner would not admit he was A.A. Austin the killer, but the detective took his response to as close to a confession as he was going to get.

Changing the subject, Philbrick asked him why he had registered at the Queen City Hotel in the past week under three different names, J. Alsop, J. Allen, and J. Olson, and yet never changed rooms? Curious, too, that he chose the name of Olson, the same name as the woman murdered in Duluth. Alsop claimed he wrote the same name every time, but that his handwriting was not clear and obviously misread.

Because his memorandum book specifically mentioned that he roomed at Guimond's Minneapolis boarding house, Courtney sought his comment on meeting his former landlady at Minnehaha Falls. Alsop, who still harbored resentment, said, "One Sunday in August '94, just prior to the Olson murder, I went from Minneapolis to Minnehaha and met two women on a streetcar whom I knew and showed them around the falls. I went downhill to the falls and met the boarding house mistress. She accosted me and demanded board money, $50, and she gave me hell. I told her I hadn't any money to pay her then, and left her walking towards the falls." He did not specify the names of the two women on the streetcar, one of whom was most likely Lena Olson.

Alsop spent the remainder of the afternoon in lonely isolation. However, he did have one visitor, a man who served him divorce papers, which undoubtedly affected his demeanor. Courtney stopped in to see Alsop, noting that his unshaven face had become deadly pale. His uncombed hair in front no longer concealed his baldness. "His nerve is breaking, and he will be ready to confess soon," thought Courtney.[33]

The prisoner, who was looking at his hands, said, "I wish you would get me that little fingernail cleaner I had when searched." His request for that small knife put Courtney on edge. As he was leaving the jail, Courtney tried to cheer up Alsop. "Keep a stiff upper lip, Jim, I will bring anything you want."

As a matter of caution, Courtney conferred with Seattle authorities regarding Alsop's state of mind. The detective was afraid that the prisoner may commit suicide and should be watched by a special guard. His fears were thought unmerited, and no more attention was given to the matter.

At eight p.m., the night jailer W.I. Peer entered Alsop's cell on his evening rounds. In an easy-going manner, Alsop queried, "By the way, do you keep on steam all night?"

"Yes," said Peer.

Looking at his jailer, he added, "It got pretty chilly last night." Although the room temperature was then comfortable, Peer checked to see if Alsop had a blanket before leaving.

The jailer gave no further attention to his detainee until ten-twenty p.m. when Courtney returned to the station with a bag of oranges. "Will you let me see Alsop?" he requested. "Certainly," replied Peer, as he got up and went after the jail keys. Then he opened the door into the women's department and entered a large cell that opened into two other smaller cells. Alsop had been placed in the cell on the left. Peer turned the key and stepped inside. The room was pitch-dark and silent.

With the illumination from the outer cell, Peer could make out that the bunk, which was on the left-hand side, was empty. "Where in the devil is Alsop?" he muttered to Courtney. After lighting a gas lamp, the flash of the flame revealed a horrible sight that took away the breath of both men. Wedged between the bunkbed's footboard and sink was the body of the coward hanging by a handmade rope.

Rushing to the man, Courtney observed that his face was partly turned to one side, and around his stretched-out neck was a rope made of plaited strips torn from his blanket. Alsop had fastened the rope to an iron bolt on the wall approximately five feet above the floor.[34] The nearly six-foot-tall man compensated for the distance by folding his legs up behind his body. His knees almost touched the floor.

The body, still warm in all its ghastliness, twisted slightly. Courtney cried, "He is still alive!"

Peer barked, "Cut him down!" Withdrawing a knife, Courtney severed the corded noose. Frantically carrying him to the middle of the cell's floor, Peer knelt down and checked for a pulse, then tried to listen for a heartbeat. "It's no use," he said, "the man is dead." In the days ahead, Courtney told a reporter:

> *What a different expression there was on the face of Alsop than when he walked into Chief Rogers' office the afternoon before. Then he showed vigor. His walk gave the impression of determination, and his face bore an expression of injured innocence. As he lay on the floor signs of worriment were visible, and a sort of haggardness, increased by a certain sallowness of complexion could be noticed. The mouth was partly open. It seemed as if he wore false teeth. His eyes were half-closed. He had taken off his black coat and vest and silk hat and placed them on the bunk over the one in which he slept. His shoes had also been removed. When Coroner Askam arrived the cell was searched, but not a thing was discovered that conveyed one idea from the dead.*

With the death of Alsop, Courtney raced downtown and wired his Minneapolis department that his prisoner had cheated the gallows. In a statement to the press, the detective said, "I am satisfied that the dead man before us is not only guilty of the murder of Lena Olson, but nine or ten others. ... I feel very sorry about his committing suicide, because I wanted him to be tried in Duluth and convicted."

Learning that her husband had committed suicide reportedly sent Mrs. Alsop into hysterics. *The Seattle Post-Intelligencer* wrote, "Mrs. Alsop is a deserving woman and has the sympathy of a large circle of friends in her present misfortune. The widow of the accused man feels the unpleasant notoriety of her position and the disgrace attached to the name she bears most keenly. Alsop left her with the care of his sixteen-year-old daughter, besides her own child by her first marriage. ... Her associates speak well of her in every way."[35]

Butterworth funeral home chapel, Seattle, Washington, 1900. Courtesy of wikimedia.org.

Duluth's Detective Benson, who had worked so hard trying to crack the case, almost fainted upon hearing the news. "I was eating breakfast on the train on my way to Minneapolis when a newsboy came through with a paper of that morning. I purchased one, and in his handing it to me my eyes caught the headlines: 'Dead!—James B. Allsop [*sic*] Commits Suicide in his Cell at Seattle'. I dropped everything. I can say I did not eat any more at that meal."[36]

The body was removed to Butterworth's undertaking parlors. The proprietor, Edgar R. Butterworth, who was credited with coining the terms "mortuary" and "mortician," operated the establishment with his five sons. Alsop, as cold and lifeless as Lena Olson had been following her demise, was placed on a slab for examination. It was discovered that there was a four-inch scar on the left side, between the first and second ribs. Mostly likely the old wound was made from a knife and healed after being stitched up. A number of photographs were taken as well.

CHAPTER NINE
Unearthing the Past

And like the morbid curiosity that followed the murder of Olson, numerous people called every day at the morgue to see whether it was the same James E. Alsop they had known. More than a dozen spectators agreed it was indeed him. A Mr. T.J. Fleetwood, a well-known Tacoma merchant, said he met him by chance in Kansas City, Missouri, on September 7, 1894. The date corresponded with Alsop's memorandum notebook. Once the nation found out that the wicked man was dead, stories abounded of where he had been in the years leading up to his arrest.

Alsop had traveled to places like New York, Wyoming, Colorado, and Utah where family members were located—finding hiding among friends most suitable. Relatives in rural Sandy, Utah, recalled he first appeared in June 1895. It had been over ten years since their last meeting back in Kansas. Alsop told them that he was widowed and that all of his children were dead. In reality, only his eldest son, John, had died of smallpox in January 1889. The pretended plight aroused their sorrow and sympathy, which evoked extended hospitality.

To the Sandy clan, Alsop appeared free from care or worry, a happy man going about his own affairs. He gave the impression that he might resume his old business of real estate, perhaps in Utah. Alsop spent the summer months tending to his sickly sixty-year-old cousin, Thomas Hill Allsop (he had retained the double "*l*" in his surname). Thomas's daughter, thirty-four-year-old Emma Allsop Dobbs of Salt Lake City, said of her cousin James: "I have never seen a man who seemed to have a more amiable disposition. He took care of my father during his last sickness, and I must say I never saw a man so gentle in the sick room. There was nothing he would not do."

Before Thomas passed away on August 30, 1895, cousin James prepared the man's final will and signed as a subscribing witness. Thomas divided the bulk of the $6,000 estate between his first wife, Elizabeth, and her children, including Dobbs. To his second or polygamous wife, Mary, he left her $1.00: "That in 1888 she left his bed and board and married two other men and raised a family of six children."

After Thomas's death, James Alsop relocated to Salt Lake City where he was welcomed at Dobbs's residence. Her husband John had deserted her and their four children in May 1893. Subsequently she filed for divorce in July 1895. Alsop remained off and on at the Dobbs's home until the spring of 1896.

Dobbs recalled that Alsop "lived a very quiet way and as far as known, made but few acquaintances." She added, "[H]e never appeared to have anything on his mind, and never seemed melancholy about anything, as it seems to me a man who committed murder must have been, but on the contrary, he was always cheerful and went about singing as though he was the happiest man in the world."

Others who became acquainted with Alsop during this time described him as a gentleman and an exceedingly fine fellow. However, the men at firehouse No. 2 remembered talking with Alsop on various occasions. To them he appeared rather peculiar and a braggart, according to a *Salt Lake Herald* interview:

> *He was always telling about his property, how much he owned at San Diego and in other places and would often appear abstracted, jumping from one topic to another with no connection between them; at one time he was going into the insurance business and had come round to make the acquaintance and at another he intended to open a real estate office. The firemen paid but little attention to his vagaries and thought him some harmless crank who come out from the east and whose brain had become affected by the altitude.*

A fortune-teller not unlike "Madame Austin" of Salt Lake City, Utah, who spiritually guided A.A. Austin in his desire to find and marry a rich wife. Courtesy of Author.

While in the capital city, Alsop also became familiar with a fortune-teller who strangely enough bore the name of Austin, his murderous alias. Over the course of several months, he visited Madame Austin's parlor, regularly seeking consultation on his one true desire—to find and marry a rich wife. She mused that he often rushed breathlessly into her place, seeking immediate answers. Described as a bulky woman without a superabundance of charms, the medium gave an interview on April 24, 1896, to the *Salt Lake Tribune*:

> *He was a handsome man, and dressed in the most fashionable clothing, which was always spick-and-span in its newness. He wore a silk hat and his shirt-front was ornamented by two diamonds. His tie, always of white lawn, gave him a ministerial appearance that was accentuated by the student-like pallor of his countenance. But in spite of his appearance and conversation, which was that of a gentleman, I never could get over an unaccountable feeling of aversion for him. I never liked his open search for a rich wife, anyway, and though he repeatedly asked me to introduce him to some nice girl who had money, I invariably declined to do so.*

> *"If a woman only had $200," he often said, "I would be satisfied. I could get to Europe, where I have $20,000 awaiting me. I wouldn't care what a woman's past was so long as she acted right while my wife." He was so persistent that in derision I dubbed him "The Millionaire," which rather pleased him when he heard of it. One day he came to me and told me he had met a blonde clerk who had struck his fancy. "Look at the cards," said he, "and see if she has money." I did so and found that she was entirely dependent upon her own exertions. Alsop dropped her without ceremony.*

On one occasion when the spiritualist was telling his fortune with cards, she told him he had a wife living. Alsop became disconcerted for a moment, and his face flushed. He declared the cards lied and abruptly left. On another visit, he noticed that Madame Austin was counting a large roll of money. Before leaving, Alsop inquired if she might like to accompany him to

Brigham Young's grave, a rather steep climb. The prophetess declined what she perceived as a romantic gesture. Later, she joyfully congratulated herself on avoiding the possibility of falling victim to him.

Two days after Madame Austin's story was published, the *Salt Lake Tribune* printed in bold headlines, "Had a Salt Lake Wife. Allsop [sic] the Murderer was also a Bigamist." The sensational story suggested the recently dead arch-criminal's last mate had been none other than Emma Dobbs, his distant cousin. It was reported that upon hearing of her husband's arrest on April 16, Dobbs sent him a sum of money for his defense.

Apparently, the money was accompanied by two loving letters, which were intercepted by the Seattle police. Upon hearing of Alsop's suicide the next day, Dobbs wired the post office authorities and petitioned for the return of her correspondence, which was granted. *The San Francisco Call* opined of the faithful Salt Lake widow, "Unlike the Tacoma widow, she was not disposed to desert her erring husband when in trouble."

Of course Dobbs denied she was ever married to James E. Alsop, although she had been in correspondence with him since he left Utah in mid-March. Recently divorced, Dobbs signed using her maiden name of Allsop, hence the sordid speculation. She flatly denied sending him money or messages of affection. The last letter she sent him was mailed to the Queen City Hotel on April 16. It was this letter that she had specifically asked the Seattle post office to return.

In a *Salt Lake Herald* interview, Dobbs said, "I am inclined to the belief that it was not because he was guilty of the crime he was charged with that he committed suicide, but rather that he did it out of the despondency over the cool reception he received from his wife at Tacoma." She added: "I know the papers say he had deserted his wife, and had not supported her for three years, but they may have had troubles that no one else knew anything about, as a great many people have, and he may have determined upon trying to mend matters when he went north. I am inclined to think that meeting such a reception and then being arrested on such a charge on top of it, he became despondent and decided to be done with any further trouble in the world."

The stories of Alsop and his sordid past slowly dissipated following his suicide. After nearly two weeks had elapsed since Alsop's arrest on April 16, a decision was finally made to bury him. Interestingly, that was not unlike the time span given to bury Lena Olson the first time. The question of disposing of Alsop's body had been a much-discussed story following his suicide.

The April 19 headline in *The Seattle Post-Intelligencer* read "Nobody Wants It. The Body of Alsop to Be Buried in a Pauper's Grave." The article stated the remains were not of use to either Duluth or Minneapolis authorities and that "not a soul seems to care what becomes of the clay that concealed a moral viper." Ashamed family members, including his widow, had no desire whatsoever to claim his remains. However, a medical student solicited the undertaker for Alsop's body. His request was denied.

Officials opted to place the remains of Alsop in a soon-to-be-forgotten grave, not unlike the resting place of Lena Olson. The same newspaper crassly concluded, "In less than a week thrilling rumors will probably be afloat of how the body was stolen, or that someone made pocketbooks out of the tanned

Murderer Thomas Blanck, twenty-four, died March 21, 1895. Known as the "Jesse James of the Pacific Northwest."

skin." On April 30, the long-sought villain who made national headlines was buried at ten a.m. in the Duwamish Cemetery in Georgetown.

Situated four miles south of the city, the paupers' graveyard at the King County Hospital and Poor Farm sat on a knoll overlooking the Duwamish River. Nearby were brothels, saloons, and gambling dens—a veritable heaven for the likes of Alsop. The area was known as the "cesspool" of Seattle.

One of his eternal companions buried nearby was the condemned murderer Thomas "Michael Hogan" Blanck, twenty-four, otherwise known as the "Jesse James of the Pacific

Northwest." He acknowledged killing five or more individuals and wounding twenty others. After escaping jail, Blanck was killed by the King County sheriff's posse on March 21, 1895.

Interred at the same time as Alsop was an unknown man discovered floating in the bay two days earlier. The corpse had evidently been in the water for nearly a week, and his face was badly decomposed. An onlooker whispered, "The man was murdered. Look at the wound on the side of his head there." Like Lena Olson, the victim was displayed in the morgue for the curious to identify. With no luck, his remains were consigned to Duwamish.

For Alsop, he was buried without ceremony, devoid of family or friends mourning in attendance. No warm tears fell on his cheap coffin supplied by the county. His official burial record indicated his name as "James E. Austin"—a combination of his real and alias murdering name. Perhaps it was an unintentional mistake or a calculated one to keep body snatchers or pocketbook makers out of reach. By the morning's end, the gravedigger had tossed and tamped his final spades of soil on top of the evil Englishman. A fitting conclusion to his miserable, earthly career.

James E. Alsop was buried without ceremony without family or friends mourning in attendance. Courtesy of Old Book Illustrations.

ASHES TO THE WIND

James E. Alsop's remains did not rest in the Duwamish Cemetery for many years. In the spring of 1912, King County commissioners ordered that eight acres of graves containing nearly 3,300 remains were to be exhumed and cremated later that fall for the purpose of creating space for a dozen factories. A crematorium was erected on-site beforehand for the burning of unclaimed bodies. According to records, only 855 had dates and names on their wooden headboards.

The American Contracting Company, which held the contract, was later cited by a grand jury in June 1913 for their shoddy documentation, disposal of remains, and billing. With implications of graft, the inadequate crematorium could only handle four bodies per day, yet the county was billed for eighty-three cremations per day for thirty-nine days. Although no one was held personally accountable, the jury found that the commissioners failed to originally offer bids on the project. Interestingly, the county undertaker's wife held the warrants to the contract, which amounted to more than $8,000.

Reports cited that the ashes of as many as 163 bodies were raked on the floor of the crematorium and apportioned into receptacles purported to bear the names of the deceased. Unclaimed cremains were apparently unceremoniously scattered to the winds. Local lore tells that "some people remember seeing bodies thrown into the Duwamish River." The former site of the cemetery and county hospital is considered one of Seattle's most haunted locations.

Sources: Brian Calvert, "Georgetown's Haunted History Unearthed," *KOMO News*, 2013; and "Duwamish Poor Farm Cemetery Burial List," peoplelegacy.com.

Epilogue

T hirty years after the Lena Olson murder case was solved, former detective John Courtney provided his recollections for the *Minneapolis Daily Star*. In a March 4, 1926, regular guest column, Courtney's piece, "A Woman's Hunch Put Me on Track of Murderer Year After Crime," offered a final glimpse into the nearly completely forgotten crime by that time.

Whether or not his memory was failing him, he took liberties with retelling the story, sensationalizing aspects that bordered on fiction. Disregarding that the murder took place in 1894, not 1895, and that Lena Olson did not own or operate a laundry (although another Lena Olson in Minneapolis did), Courtney's insights at least contained a personal perspective, which until then were unpublished:

> *I remember way back when Lena Olson, who conducted a hand laundry here in Minneapolis, was lured by a huge psychopathic freak to what was known as "The Point" in Lake Superior at Duluth, strangled to death, and covered with sand, only to serve later as mute testimony of a romance hideously broken almost at its very inception.*

> *For years she'd washed and ironed, washed and ironed, dreaming always of the days when some Lockinvar [fictional romantic hero*

of the ballad "Marmion" (1808) by Sir Walter Scott] would ... take her away from the drudgery. Toward the last she wondered if it always would be her fate to slave that way.

And just when she was wondering, along came a man, not the Lockinvar she had been dreaming about, but a big mountain of a man six feet two inches tall and weighing nearly 250 pounds [apparently James E. Alsop gained three inches and seventy-five pounds since 1896]. There was a kind of fierce look about him, but he had a certain way that fascinated her, and his requests were as good as orders in the little mind so long fixed on just plain drudgery.

That's why, when finally, he said he wanted to take her to Duluth and get married, she unquestionably sold the hand laundry, took all her money out of the bank, packed her trunk, and her grips, and got on the train with him for the land of her dreams. Any place away from the hand laundry was the "Land of Dreams."[37]

Former Minneapolis Detective John J. Courtney. Courtesy of Newspapers.com.

Courtney continued with Alsop's brutalizing Olson and then leaving her body on the shore of Minnesota Point. He did not mention Zenith City's Detective Benson's year-and-a-half struggle to find the murderer. However, he did write about his involvement

John J. Courtney business card. Posted on October 16, 2018, Reddit.com: "I found this business card in the wall of my house built in 1908." Courtesy of Reddit.com.

in the case that commenced in the spring of 1896, which began with an unrelated holdup:

> *I was on the Minneapolis detective force at the time of the holdup and therefore had occasion to go to northeast Minneapolis to interview a woman in a certain case in court. After the business was disposed of, the woman [Mrs. Guimond] informed me that a big, strapping man had stopped at her home about a year before and had suddenly disappeared, leaving his grip which apparently contained valuable papers. The papers included a will signed by the name Alsop. I wasn't interested at first, but the woman seemed to have a "hunch" that Alsop was the Olson [sic. A.A. Austin] wanted in Duluth and that did make me sit up.*
>
> *The result was a letter to the police chief in Duluth who promptly sent down the signature from the hotel register. One glance at this and at the writing on the will revealed them to be identical. There was no doubt about the matter whatever. I hurried to Duluth, but could only corroborate information already obtained that Alsop once lived in Tacoma.*

Going there [to Tacoma] ... I got in touch at last with a young attorney who knew something of the Alsops and seemed to think he could trail down the man. Of course I didn't say that I wanted him on a murder charge, but I did offer a reward of $100 for the correct address. That offer was the one thing needed to wind up the case. The attorney got busy and located Mrs. Alsop in almost no time. This in turn led to the information that Alsop had been at the home only a few days before and had gone into the [Minnesota] "mining country."

His address, he had said, would be general delivery, Seattle. The general delivery window in Seattle naturally was the place I headed for and in less than a day I had my man, said to be quite a well-to-do land operator. He took the arrest coolly enough, but after he got locked up, asked me for a penknife to clean his fingernails.

I didn't give it to him and warned the police chief that the man would commit suicide. He was found hanging in his cell the next morning. Thus was Lena Olson avenged more than a year after the terrible crime. The county commissioners in Duluth gave me a reward of $250. The state also rewarded me [$250].

Within the year, Courtney passed away on November 1, 1926, in Minneapolis at the age of sixty-five. Born in Kerry County, Ireland, in 1861, Courtney had made Minnesota his home for forty-four years. He had led an interesting and colorful life, including a decade on the police force.

In February 1897, less than one year after solving the Olson case, he had an altercation with a woman proprietor of a bath parlor on Washington Avenue. Courtney was charged with conduct unbecoming an officer and a gentleman, and the mayor demanded his resignation, which was tendered immediately. In the years following, he married twice, fathered two sons, operated various saloons and pool rooms, and dabbled in real estate.

After Courtney's death, the Olson case completely faded away from public memory.

And for those who were connected to the investigation from 1894–1896, several suffered the same fate, either living their lives in relative obscurity or coming to sad endings.

Julia Alsop, the second wife of James E. Alsop, persevered in the years to come. After her husband's suicide in 1896, she followed her passion as an artist. Mrs. Alsop became prominent in the Tacoma art circles and operated her own studio. In 1908 she married fellow artist Frank A. Tabor. She died in February 1935 in Bremerton, Washington.

Duluth police chief Harry Armstrong founded the National Iron Works after leaving his post in March 1896. Becoming rather wealthy, he later moved to Laguna Beach, California, and he was recognized as one of the community's best-known citizens. In August 1931, Armstrong, seventy-five, drowned in the surf.

After his dismissal in March 1896, Detective Bob Benson operated a private agency in Duluth for several years and also invested in local real estate tracts funded primarily by his wife Saloma. In April 1902, he vanished, leaving her penniless and distraught. By the summer of 1904, she was unable to locate him and consequently sued for divorce claiming desertion.

The sordid affair made headlines in the city's newspapers for several months, exposing him for forging deeds and absconding with proceeds from the sale of property partly or fully owned by her. Some speculated that he had eloped with his stenographer and later died somewhere out west (before 1918). One report said he was shot to death in St. Louis.

Benson's Detective Agency

TELEPHONE 650.

I am fully prepared to undertake any work in my line of a legitimate nature. (No divorse cases handled). Correspondence solicited and given prompt attention. All matters intrusted to me will be treated strictly confidential. Call, address or wire

ROBT. A. BENSON,

13 and 14 American Exchange Bank Bldg., Duluth, Minn., Cor. 3d Av. W & Sup. st.

After being fired from the Duluth Police Department, Bob Benson opened his own detective agency, March 1896. Courtesy of the Minnesota Historical Society Newspaper Digital Hub.

Claus Blixt, the henchman employed by Harry Hayward in the death of Kitty Ging, died at the age of seventy-two in Stillwater Prison on August 21, 1925—thirty-one years to the day when Lena Olson was murdered. Convicted of a life sentence in 1895, Blixt remained an interest to newspaper readers for the remainder of his life. In 1906, several family members, who had grown weary of the case's notoriety and familial association, petitioned the courts for a name change from Blixt to Johnston. The following year a rumor circulated that Blixt had engineered a plot to blow up the prison by allowing the water in the boiler to get too low. The warden quickly refuted the story, but not before it was circulated in print. Reportedly, Blixt "went insane" while incarcerated.

Guy Browning, the boy who discovered Olson's body on O-at-ka Beach, faced hardship in his early years. His father died in 1903 at the age of fifty from a massive stroke, leaving him the "man of the house." In order to help support his widowed mother and three sisters, he worked at the shipyards. When Browning was eighteen years old, he headed west in the summer of 1906 to Cabinet, Idaho. There he found a job with the railroad but tragically died on November 23 as a result of a workplace accident that occurred two days earlier. He was buried in the Greenwood Cemetery (St. Louis County Poor Farm).

St. Louis County Coroner Dr. John J. Eklund, a noted surgeon who later became one of the most prominent and influential citizens of Duluth, was shot to death in his office in April 1922. His assailant turned the gun on himself and committed suicide.[38]

After resigning in March 1896, Duluth junior detective Tom Hayden operated a saloon in town. In 1898 he relocated to Seattle, where he served for many years in the police department.

Lizzie Olson, the younger sister of Lena, was remembered as tenacious in her desire to bring the villainous J.E. Alsop, alias A.A. Austin, to justice. She never married, and the drudgery of servant work continued for her into the 1930s, where she earned her pay as a laundress for a family in Minneapolis. On her seventy-third birthday, February 13, 1941, she was admitted to Rochester State Hospital, a facility to treat mental illness. The last surviving person with intimate knowledge of one of the most notorious cases of the late nineteenth century, Olson took her final breath at approximately ten forty-five in the morning, February 2, 1944. Her death certificate stated she died of complications of senility.

Acknowledgments

O ver the course of the last decade, numerous individuals and organizations assisted me as I developed my manuscript. In January 2019, I shared the initial pages of my then-titled manuscript *Murder at Minnesota Point: A Faithful Retelling of the Sensational Nationwide Manhunt for a Serial Killer* with nearly two-dozen people. The overwhelming response was one of encouragement to continue with the project. My thanks to the following first readers who offered feedback: Lynette Anderson, Amy Azinger and family, Kristell Benson, Amy Boxrud, Kevin Dunn, Theresa Duchene, Cleo Granneman, Jennifer Huebscher, Jeanie Klasen, Mike Kooiman, Maddie Moskal, Mike Novak, Jeanie Owens, Ben Paulson, Julie Rappe, Doug Rock, Eileen Shimota and family, Jack Q. Smith, Jane Weis, and Mona Weselmann.

I also owe a great deal of gratitude to Dale Hovland, volunteer extraordinaire at the Norwegian-American Historical Association, Northfield, Minnesota. Working closely together for many years, I benefited from his unfailing support in unearthing telling clippings, conducting research, and translating materials when needed.

Upon Hovland's suggestion in the summer of 2020, I contacted The Gilbertsville Free Library, Gilbertsville, New York.

Within two weeks of posting my letter, I received a call from the library archivist, Leigh Eckmair. How I remember that fascinating hour we shared on the phone. At the time I was visiting relatives in southwestern Minnesota and took notes on the back of an envelope while sitting in the car. After our conversation, a packet of photocopied items related to James E. Alsop arrived. Since our initial contact, Eckmair's interest in my project has remained steadfast.

Other historical societies and institutions have also been incredibly helpful and courteous, including: Marjean Deines, Director, Trego County Historical Society, WaKeeney, Kansas; Aimee Brown, Archivist and Curator of Special Collections, University of Minnesota Duluth, Kathryn A. Martin Library, Northeast Minnesota Historical Collections, Duluth, Minnesota; Duluth Public Library Reference Department, Duluth, Minnesota; Tony Dierckins, Zenith City Press, Duluth, Minnesota; and the Kitsap Historical Society & Museum, Bremerton, Washington.

As with any involved writing project, friends and family got caught up in the narrative over the course of the years it took to write this story. My dear friend Juleen Trisko-Schneider was concerned about my wellbeing in pursuing this project, posing good questions, and reminding me to honor Lena Olson's memory and not cast her as a victim lost to history.

My stalwart cheerleaders included Amy Azinger and Eileein Shimota, who were always ready at hand to help and offer ideas. The late Professor Qiguang Zhao, who proved a good listener and friend. Lynette Anderson, my lovely sister, is a mystery aficionado and was always asking to hear the latest about my book. Her infectious excitement gave me confidence to proceed with telling the story. My sons, Bailey and Holden Sauve, regularly put up with me taking them to cemeteries, my endless chatter about the latest plot development, and the set-backs or progress experienced. Holden's fiance Taylor Wicklund was always supportive and asked many questions to encourage me.

My partner and talented editor, Evelyn Hoover—this book is as much yours as it is mine. You have listened repeatedly to me telling the story to countless individuals who wanted to learn more. You helped me frame, write, edit, and revise this manuscript. I believe this book brought us closer together as we sat huddled over my laptop many a Saturday morning reviewing changes and making edits. Thank you for your patience and loving support.

Finally, I want to acknowledge the professional work of the great team at Red Line Editorial, without whom this book would not be possible. Proceeds from the book will benefit a fitting memorial stone to be placed at Lena's grave. It is my way of commemorating a life that was cut short but is not forgotten.

Bibliography

"1894 $500 Murder Reward Wanted Poster For A.A. Austin."
Worthpoint.com. Accessed Jan. 10, 2021. https://www.worthpoint.com/
worthopedia/1894-500-murder-reward-wanted-poster-73938803.

"A Couple of Women Bearing ..." *Western Kansas World,* WaKeeney, KS,
March 12, 1887, 4. Accessed Feb. 23, 2021. https://chroniclingamerica.loc.
gov/.

"A Fiend!" *Minneapolis Tribune*, April 26, 1896, 1. Minnesota Historical
Society, St. Paul, MN. Minnesota Newspaper Digital Hub. Accessed
March 3, 2021. https://newspapers.mnhs.org/jsp/browse.jsp.

"After Lena Olson's Murderer." *Duluth News Tribune*, January 16, 1895, 2.
Accessed Nov. 7, 2012. https://www.newsbank.com/.

"Is All a Mystery." *Duluth News Tribune*, August 23, 1894, 1. Accessed Nov.
7, 2012. https://www.newsbank.com/.

"Alsop, Mary I. Hollis." Source unknown, ca. November 1890. Clipping
found in local history collection scrapbook #S-5-69 kept by Florence
Stebbins, The Gilbertsville Free Library, Gilbertsville, NY.

"Alsop Known Here." *Salt Lake Herald*, April 22, 1896, 8. Accessed Nov.
27, 2021. https://chroniclingamerica.loc.gov/.

"Alsop, Without Doubt." *Minneapolis Tribune*, April 28, 1896, 5.
Minnesota Historical Society, St. Paul, MN. Minnesota Newspaper Digital
Hub. Accessed March 3, 2021. https://newspapers.mnhs.org/jsp/browse.
jsp.

"Among the Finest." Source unknown, ca. April 1895. Northeast
Minnesota Historical Center, University of Minnesota-Duluth.
Collection: Duluth (City) Police Department Records.

"Another Austin Found." *Duluth Evening Herald*, October 18, 1894, 3. Minnesota Historical Society, St. Paul, MN. Minnesota Newspaper Digital Hub. Accessed March 3, 2021. https://newspapers.mnhs.org/jsp/browse. jsp.

"Another Austin Found. An Ohio Sheriff Thinks He Has the Murderer." *Duluth Evening Herald*, February 15, 1896, 6. Minnesota Historical Society, St. Paul, MN. Minnesota Newspaper Digital Hub. Accessed March 3, 2021. https://newspapers.mnhs.org/jsp/browse.jsp.

"Another Body Found." *Duluth Evening Herald*, September 10, 1894, 2. Minnesota Historical Society, St. Paul, MN. Minnesota Newspaper Digital Hub. Accessed Dec. 10, 2020. https://newspapers.mnhs.org/jsp/browse.jsp.

Archives of The Gilbertsville Free Library, Gilbertsville, NY: Local History Collection.

Archives of the Kitsap County Historical Society & Museum, Bremerton, WA: Jesse C. Jones Archives.

Archives of Northeast Minnesota Historical Center, University of Minnesota-Duluth, Duluth, Minnesota Collection: Duluth (City) Police Department Records.

Archives of the Norwegian-American Historical Association, St. Olaf College, Northfield, MN.

"Arthur Austin. Was Arrested in New Orleans. Charged with Lena Olson's Murder." *Duluth News Tribune,* December 15, 1894, 1. Accessed Nov. 7, 2012. https://www.newsbank.com/.

"A Telegram received." Source unknown, annotated date: "November 24, 1890." Clipping found in local history collection scrapbook #S-5-69 kept by Florence Stebbins, The Gilbertsville Free Library, Gilbertsville, NY.

"A Terrible Death." *Western Kansas World*, WaKeeney, KS, December 6, 1890, 4. Accessed Feb. 23, 2021. https://chroniclingamerica.loc.gov/.

"Attempts Suicide in Jail." *The Seattle Post-Intelligencer,* May 5, 1900, 5. Accessed March 1, 2021. https://chroniclingamerica.loc.gov/.

"Austin. Claus Blixt Says He Was Undoubtedly Killed by Harry Hayward." *Duluth Evening Herald*, December 12, 1895, 1. Minnesota Historical Society, St. Paul, MN. Minnesota Newspaper Digital Hub. Accessed Feb. 8, 2020. https://newspapers.mnhs.org/jsp/browse.jsp.

"Austin Hangs Himself." *Duluth News Tribune*, April 18, 1896, 1, 3. Accessed Nov. 7, 2012. https://www.newsbank.com/.

"Austin Captured." *Duluth Evening Herald*, April 17, 1896, 1. Minnesota Historical Society, St. Paul, MN, Newspaper Digital Hub. Accessed Feb. 22, 2021. https://newspapers.mnhs.org/jsp/browse.jsp.

"Austin Is Captured." *Duluth Evening Herald*, October 22, 1894, 5. Minnesota Historical Society, St. Paul, MN, Minnesota Newspaper Digital Hub. Accessed Feb. 8, 2021. https://newspapers.mnhs.org/jsp/browse.jsp.

"Austin Was Here." *Duluth News Tribune*, September 15, 1894, 1. Accessed Nov. 7, 2012. https://www.newsbank.com/.

"A Villain." *Duluth Evening Herald*, April 27, 1896, 2. Minnesota Historical Society, St. Paul, MN. Minnesota Newspaper Digital Hub. Accessed March 8, 2021. https://newspapers.mnhs.org/jsp/browse.jsp.

Bakk-Hansen, Heidi. "The Slaying of Dr. J.J. Eklund." zenithcity.com. Accessed Nov. 1, 2021.

"Barron Is Insane." *The Seattle Post-Intelligencer,* May 6, 1900, 18. Accessed March 1, 2021. https://chroniclingamerica.loc.gov/.

"Bears Are Numerous." *Duluth Evening Herald*, August 13, 1894, 6. Minnesota Historical Society, St. Paul, MN, Minnesota Newspaper Digital Hub. Accessed Dec. 10, 2020. https://newspapers.mnhs.org/jsp/browse. jsp.

Bergland, Betty A. and Lori Ann Lahlum, eds. *Norwegian American Women: Migration, Communities, and Identities.* St. Paul: Minnesota Historical Society, 2011.

"Boys on a Bum." *Western Kansas World,* WaKeeney, KS, May 28, 1887, 5. Accessed Feb. 23, 2021. https://chroniclingamerica.loc.gov/.

Calvert, Brian. "Georgetown's Haunted History Unearthed." *KOMO News*, Seattle, WA, posted March 6, 2013. Accessed March 3, 2021. komonews. com.

Carlson, Christine. "The Historic Battle that Ended at Neiashi/Mn. Point—Part Seven," *Nahgahchiwanong Dibahjimowinnan* (August 2015). Accessed Dec. 21, 2020. https://fdlrez.com/.

"Caught on the Run." *Duluth News Tribune*, June 10, 1901, 4. Accessed Dec. 29, 2020. https://www.newsbank.com/.

"Certain It Was She." *Duluth News Tribune*, September 9, 1894, 1. Accessed Nov. 7, 2012. https://www.newsbank.com/.

"Charged with Double Murder." *The San Francisco Call,* April 17, 1896, 3. Accessed March 3, 2021. https://chroniclingamerica.loc.gov/.

"City Briefs." *Duluth Evening Herald*, Aug. 2, 1893, 6. Minnesota Historical Society, St. Paul, MN. Minnesota Newspaper Digital Hub. Accessed Dec. 1, 2021. https://newspapers.mnhs.org/jsp/browse.jsp.

"Cleverly Trapped." *Minneapolis Tribune*, January 21, 1895, 5. Minnesota Historical Society, St. Paul, MN. Minnesota Newspaper Digital Hub. Accessed Nov. 12, 2020. https://newspapers.mnhs.org/jsp/browse.jsp.

Courtney, John J. "A Woman's Hunch Put Me on Track of Murderer Year After Crime." *Minneapolis Daily Star*, March 4, 1926, 7. Accessed Aug. 15, 2020. https://www.newspapers.com/.

"Craven!" *Minneapolis Tribune*, April 19, 1896, 5. Minnesota Historical Society, St. Paul, MN. Minnesota Newspaper Digital Hub. Accessed Jan. 8, 2021. https://newspapers.mnhs.org/jsp/browse.jsp.

"Dashed to Death." Source unknown, ca. November 1890. Clipping found in local history collection scrapbook #S-5-69 kept by Florence Stebbins, The Gilbertsville Free Library, Gilbertsville, NY.

"Dead!" *Minneapolis Tribune*, April 18, 1896, 1. Minnesota Historical Society, St. Paul, MN. Minnesota Newspaper Digital Hub. Accessed Feb. 22, 2021. https://newspapers.mnhs.org/jsp/browse.jsp.

"Death of William Alsop." Source unknown, annotated "April 18, 1886." Clipping found in local history collection scrapbook #S-12-69 kept by Florence Stebbins, The Gilbertsville Free Library, Gilbertsville, NY.

"Desperate Bob Benson Assaults the Editor of The Citizen." *Duluth Citizen,* June 6, 1896, 1. Accessed Feb. 4, 2021. https://newspaperarchive.com/.

"Detective Benson. A Private Detective Agency Opened in Exchange Building." *Duluth Evening Herald,* March 26, 1896, 8. Minnesota Historical Society, St. Paul, MN. Minnesota Newspaper Digital Hub. Accessed Feb. 17, 2021. https://newspapers.mnhs.org/jsp/browse.jsp.

Duwamish Poor Farm Cemetery Burial List. Accessed March 3, 2021. https://peoplelegacy.com/.

El-Hai, Jack. "The Killer Who Haunts Me." *Minnesota Monthly* (February 2010): 58-63. Minnesota Historical Society, St. Paul, MN. Accessed Nov. 16, 2021. https://www.minnesotamonthly.com/.

"English As She Is Wrote." *Duluth Evening Herald*, July 10, 1889, 1. Minnesota Historical Society, St. Paul, MN. Minnesota Newspaper Digital Hub. Accessed Feb. 5, 2021. https://newspapers.mnhs.org/jsp/browse.jsp.

"Established a Bath House." *Duluth Evening Herald*, June 26, 1894, 3. Minnesota Historical Society, St. Paul, MN. Minnesota Newspaper Digital Hub. Accessed Dec. 30, 2020. https://newspapers.mnhs.org/jsp/browse. jsp.

"Flashes of the Past. Letter to the Journal (written in 1884)." *Otsego Journal,* Gilbertsville, NY, Oct. 1, 1942. Clipping found in local history collection. Alsop file, The Gilbertsville Free Library, Gilbertsville, NY.

"Found a Floater." *The Seattle Post-Intelligencer*, April 29, 1896, 9. Accessed March 3, 2021. https://chroniclingamerica.loc.gov/.

"Found the Woman's Hat." *Duluth Evening Herald*, August 29, 1894, 6. Minnesota Historical Society, St. Paul, MN. Minnesota Newspaper Digital Hub. Accessed Dec. 9, 2020. https://newspapers.mnhs.org/jsp/browse.jsp.

"From Allsop's [sic] Diary." *Minneapolis Journal*, April 25, 1896, 6. Accessed Nov. 9, 2012. https://www.newsbank.com/. "Found a Floater." *The Seattle Post-Intelligencer,* April 29, 1896, 9. Accessed March 3, 2021. https://chroniclingamerica.loc.gov/.

Goodsell, Edward H. *Harry Hayward: Life, Crimes, Dying Confession and Execution of the Celebrated Minneapolis Criminal; Other Interesting Chapters on the Greatest Psychological Problem of the Century.* Minneapolis: Calhoun Publishing Co., 1896. Accessed March 11, 2021. https://books.google. com/.

"Green Room Gossip." *Duluth Evening Herald*, December 27, 1910, 5. Minnesota Historical Society, St. Paul, MN. Minnesota Newspaper Digital Hub. Accessed Dec. 29, 2020. https://newspapers.mnhs.org/jsp/browse. jsp.

"Has But a Single Day to Live." *Minneapolis Tribune*, December 10, 1895, 1. Minnesota Historical Society, St. Paul, MN. Minnesota Newspaper Digital Hub. Accessed Feb. 16, 2021. https://newspapers.mnhs.org/jsp/browse.jsp.

"Hayward Looks Like Him." *Minneapolis Tribune*, December 15, 1894, 7. Minnesota Historical Society, St. Paul, MN. Minnesota Newspaper Digital Hub. Accessed Nov. 26, 2012. https://newspapers.mnhs.org/jsp/browse.jsp.

"He Knew Austin Well." *Duluth News Tribune*, April 22, 1896, 4. Accessed Nov. 7, 2012. https://www.newsbank.com/.

"He Was Not Austin." *Duluth News Tribune*, September 24, 1894, 5. Accessed Dec. 16, 2020. https://www.newsbank.com/.

"Historical Locations: Campsites/Villages." *Duluth Stories*. Accessed Dec. 31, 2020. https://www.duluthstories.net/.

Hollandsworth, Skip. *The Midnight Assassin*. NY: Henry Holt, 2016.

Huch, Ronald K. " 'Typhoid' Truelsen, Water, and Politics in Duluth, 1896–1900." *Minnesota History* (Spring 1981): 189–199. Minnesota Historical Society, St. Paul, Minnesota, Minnesota. Accessed Nov 16, 2021. http://collections.mnhs.org/MNHistoryMagazine/articles/47/v47i05p189-199.pdf.

Hurd, D. Hamilton. *History of Otsego County, New York: with illustrations and biographical sketches of some of its prominent men and pioneers*. Philadelphia: Everts & Fariss, 1878. Accessed March 11, 2021. https://books.google.com/.

"Is All a Mystery," *Duluth News Tribune*, August 23, 1894, 1. Accessed Nov. 15, 2012. https://www.newsbank.com/.

"Is Chief. Iwan Hanson Donned the Star and Began Duty Today." *Duluth Evening Herald*, March 10, 1896, 6. Minnesota Historical Society, St. Paul, MN. Minnesota Newspaper Digital Hub. Accessed Feb. 17, 2021. https://newspapers.mnhs.org/jsp/browse.jsp.

"Is Not The Man." *Duluth Evening Herald*, October 23, 1894, 8. Minnesota Historical Society, St. Paul, MN. Minnesota Newspaper Digital Hub. Accessed Feb. 17, 2021. https://newspapers.mnhs.org/jsp/browse.jsp.

"Is Still a Mystery." *Duluth Evening Herald*, August 24, 1894, 8. Minnesota Historical Society, St. Paul, MN. Minnesota Newspaper Digital Hub. Accessed Nov. 1, 2013. https://newspapers.mnhs.org/jsp/browse.jsp.

"Is Surely the Man." *Duluth News Tribune*, February 20, 1896, 4. Accessed Nov. 7, 2012. https://www.newsbank.com/.

"Is Very Insane." *Duluth Evening Herald*, April 13, 1896, 6. Minnesota Historical Society, St. Paul, MN. Minnesota Newspaper Digital Hub. Accessed March 3, 2021. https://newspapers.mnhs.org/jsp/browse.jsp.

"It Is Not Austin." *Duluth News Tribune,* February 22, 1896, 5. Accessed Nov. 15, 2012. https://www.newsbank.com/.

"It would indeed be funny ..." *Duluth News Tribune*, April 17, 1896, 2. Accessed Nov. 15, 2012. https://www.newsbank.com/.

Janvier, Thomas A. "A Duluth Tragedy." *Harper's New Monthly Magazine* (August 1899): 402–421. Accessed Dec. 17, 2020. https://www.unz.com/.

"J.E. Alsop." *Western Kansas World,* WaKeeney, KS, August 6, 1887, 2. Accessed Feb. 23, 2021. https://chroniclingamerica.loc.gov/.

"Just Like a Woman." *Minneapolis Tribune*, October 13, 1894, 5. Minnesota Historical Society, St. Paul, MN. Minnesota Newspaper Digital Hub. Accessed Jan. 8, 2021. https://newspapers.mnhs.org/jsp/browse.jsp.

"Killed Her Child. Awful Crime of Lena Olson, a Domestic at Magee's Restaurant. Betrayed and Abandoned." *St. Paul Daily Globe*, March 23, 1895, 1. Minnesota Historical Society, St. Paul, MN. Minnesota Newspaper Digital Hub. Accessed Feb. 16, 2021. https://newspapers.mnhs.org/jsp/browse.jsp.

"Know His Face." *Duluth News Tribune*, January 20, 1895, 1. Accessed Nov. 9, 2012. https://www.newsbank.com/.

Lakewood Cemetery Funeral and Grave Search, Lakewood Cemetery, Minneapolis, MN. Accessed March 19, 2021. https://www.lakewoodcemetery.org/burial-search/.

Larson, Erik. *The Devil in the White City: Murder, Magic, and Madness at the Fair That Changed America.* NY: Crown Publishing Group, 2002.

"Last Friday Night, Geo. Brooks ..." *Western Kansas World,* March 5, 1887, 4. Accessed Feb. 23, 2021. https://chroniclingamerica.loc.gov/.

"Lena Olson's Money." *Minneapolis Tribune*, September 16, 1894, 7. Minnesota Historical Society, St. Paul, MN. Minnesota Newspaper Digital Hub. Accessed Jan. 8, 2021. https://newspapers.mnhs.org/jsp/browse.jsp.

"Lena Olson's Murder." *Duluth Evening Herald*, December 10, 1894, 5. Minnesota Historical Society, St. Paul, MN. Minnesota Newspaper Digital Hub. Accessed Feb. 8, 2021. https://newspapers.mnhs.org/jsp/browse.jsp.

Levingston, Steven. *Little Demon in the City of Light: A True Story of Murder and Mesmerism in Belle Époque Paris.* NY: Doubleday, 2014.

Lydecker, Ryck and Lawrence J. Sommer, eds. *Duluth: Sketches of the Past. A Bicentennial Collection.* Duluth: American Revolution Bicentennial Commission, 1976.

"Madame Austin's Story." *Salt Lake Tribune*, April 22, 1896, 8. Accessed March 3, 2021. https://www.newspapers.com/.

"May Hinder Identification." *Duluth Evening Herald*, September 1, 1894, 6. Minnesota Historical Society, St. Paul, MN. Minnesota Newspaper Digital Hub. Accessed Dec. 21, 2020. https://newspapers.mnhs.org/jsp/browse.jsp.

McClary, Daryl C. "Condemned Murderer Thomas Blanck Escapes from the King County Jail on March 17, 1895." Historylink.org, essay 9391, posted May 12, 2010. Accessed March 3, 2021. https://www.historylink.org/.

Minnesota Historical Society, St. Paul, MN: Minnesota Death Records (1904–2001). Accessed Dec. 17, 2020. https://www.mnhs.org/research.

"Mrs. Dobbs Alleges Desertion." Salt Lake Herald, July 23, 1895, 5. Accessed March 1, 2021. https://chroniclingamerica.loc.gov/.

"Murdered for Money." *The Seattle Post-Intelligencer,* September 4, 1893, 2. Accessed March 1, 2021. https://chroniclingamerica.loc.gov/.

"Murderer Is Known." *St. Paul Daily Globe,* September 23, 1894, 2. Minnesota Historical Society, St. Paul, MN. Minnesota Newspaper Digital Hub. Accessed Jan. 8, 2021. https://newspapers.mnhs.org/jsp/browse.jsp.

"Mystery on Mystery." *Duluth News Tribune*, August 28, 1894, 1. Accessed May 16, 2013. https://www.newsbank.com/.

"New Clues." *Duluth News Tribune,* December 14, 1894, 8. Accessed Nov. 7, 2012. https://www.newsbank.com/.

"Nobody Wants It." *The Seattle Post-Intelligencer,* April 19, 1896, 8. Accessed March 3, 2021. https://chroniclingamerica.loc.gov/.

"No improper characters." *Duluth Evening Herald*, July 6, 1889, 3-4. Minnesota Historical Society, St. Paul, MN. Minnesota Newspaper Digital Hub. Accessed Dec. 29, 2020. https://newspapers.mnhs.org/jsp/browse. jsp.

"Notes." *Duluth Evening Herald*, July 9, 1889, 1. Minnesota Historical Society, St. Paul, MN. Minnesota Newspaper Digital Hub. Accessed Feb. 5, 2021. https://newspapers.mnhs.org/jsp/browse.jsp.

"Not the Right Man." *Minneapolis Tribune*, January 22, 1895, 5. Accessed Nov. 21, 2012. https://www.newsbank.com/.

"One More Clue." *St. Paul Daily Globe,* September 10, 1894, 6. Minnesota Historical Society, St. Paul, MN. Minnesota Newspaper Digital Hub. Accessed Jan. 8, 2021. https://newspapers.mnhs.org/jsp/browse.jsp.

"Operated a 'Blind Pig'." *Duluth News Tribune*, August 23, 1892, 1. Accessed Nov. 27, 2013. https://www.newsbank.com/.

Øyane, Lars E. *Gards og Ættesoga for Luster Kommune: III Dale 2—Og Nes Sokn (The Luster County Farm and Family History Book. Volume III - Dale 2— and Nes Church Area).* Luster Kommune, Norway, 1987.

Pardee, John Stone and Woodbridge, Dwight Edwards. *History of Duluth and St. Louis County, Past and Present.* Chicago: C.F. Cooper, 1910. Accessed March 11, 2021. https://books.google.com/.

Peters, Shawn Francis. *The Infamous Harry Hayward: A True Account of Murder and Mesmerism in Gilded Age Minneapolis.* Minneapolis: University of Minnesota Press, 2018.

"Police. Some Information Concerning the Department Which Guards the Peace." *Duluth Evening Herald*, November 2, 1895, 1. Minnesota Historical Society, St. Paul, MN. Minnesota Newspaper Digital Hub. Accessed Feb. 5, 2021. https://newspapers.mnhs.org/jsp/browse.jsp.

"Positively Identified." *Duluth Evening Herald*, September 10, 1894, 2. Minnesota Historical Society, St. Paul, MN. Minnesota Newspaper Digital Hub. Accessed Jan. 12, 2021. https://newspapers.mnhs.org/jsp/browse. jsp.

"Probate Court. Will of the Late Thomas Allsop Filed For Probate."
Salt Lake Herald, May 28, 1896, 5. Accessed Nov. 27, 2021.
https://chroniclingamerica.loc.gov/.

"Proceedings of the Board of County Commissioners of St. Louis County,
Minnesota." *Duluth Evening Herald*, August 1, 1896, 10. Minnesota
Historical Society, St. Paul, MN. Minnesota Newspaper Digital Hub.
Accessed Nov. 21, 2012. https://newspapers.mnhs.org/jsp/browse.jsp.

"Proofs Are Furnished." *Duluth Evening Herald*, September 13, 1897, 5.
Minnesota Historical Society, St. Paul, MN. Minnesota Newspaper Digital
Hub. Accessed Feb. 7, 2019. https://newspapers.mnhs.org/jsp/browse.jsp.

Randolph, A.M.F., Reporter. *Reports of Cases Argued and Determined in the
Supreme Court of the State of Kansas.* Topeka, KS: Clifford C. Baker, State
Printer, 1888, 487–496. Accessed March 11, 2021. https://books.google.
com/.

"Reads Like Holmes." *The Seattle Post-Intelligencer,* April 17, 1896, 8.
Accessed March 2, 2021. https://chroniclingamerica.loc.gov/.

Recorder's Office, Ramsey County, St. Paul, MN.

"Reveled in Crime." *The Seattle Post-Intelligencer,* September 4, 1897, 8.
Accessed March 1, 2021. https://chroniclingamerica.loc.gov/.

Richardson, Frank Herbert. *Richardson's Tourists' Guide to Chicago: The
West and the Lake Superior.* Chicago: Monarch Book Co., 1904, Accessed
Dec. 17, 2020. https://books.google.com/.

"Says Lena Olson Was an Employe [*sic*] of the Historic Ozark Flats,
Where Hayward Knew Her." Source unknown, annotated date: "Dec. 12,
1895." Northeast Minnesota Historical Center, University of Minnesota-
Duluth, Duluth, MN. Collection: Duluth (City) Police Department
Records.

Sensel, Jean. *Spanaway*. West Columbia, SC: Arcadia Publishing, 2014, 42.
Accessed March 1, 2021. https://books.google.com/.

"Several Clews [*sic*]." *Duluth Evening Herald*, August 23, 1894, 8.
Minnesota Historical Society, St. Paul, MN. Minnesota Newspaper Digital
Hub. Accessed Nov. 7, 2012. https://newspapers.mnhs.org/jsp/browse.
jsp.

"She Is Still Dead." *Duluth Sunday News Tribune,* August 26, 1894, 1. Accessed Nov. 1, 2013. https://www.newsbank.com/.

Souvenir of Duluth, Minnesota. Dubuque, IA: Alexander Simplot, 1893. Accessed Dec. 29, 2020. https://mndigital.org/.

"Story of Crime From Seattle." *The San Francisco Call*, April 24, 1896, 3. Accessed March 3, 2021. https://chroniclingamerica.loc.gov/.

"Strangled to Death." *The Seattle Post-Intelligencer,* April 18, 1896, 8. Accessed March 2, 2021. https://chroniclingamerica.loc.gov/.

"Tales of The Town." *The Duluth Rip-Saw*, July 17, 1917, 2; and February 9, 1918, 2. Minnesota Historical Society, St. Paul, MN. Minnesota Newspaper Digital Hub. Accessed Feb. 17, 2021. https://newspapers. mnhs.org/jsp/browse.jsp.

"The Man Blixt Who Has Confessed." *New Ulm Review*, December 12, 1894, 5. Minnesota Historical Society, St. Paul, MN. Minnesota Newspaper Digital Hub. Accessed Feb. 8, 2021. https://newspapers.mnhs. org/jsp/browse.jsp.

"The O-at-ka Murder." *Duluth Evening Herald*, September 10, 1894, 2. Minnesota Historical Society, St. Paul, MN. Minnesota Newspaper Digital Hub. Accessed Jan. 8, 2021. https://newspapers.mnhs.org/jsp/browse.jsp.

"The Parks of Minnesota Point." Zenith City Press (online). Excerpted from Dierckins, Tony and Nancy S. Nelson. *Duluth's Historic Parks: Their First 160 Years.* Duluth, Minnesota: Zenith City Press, 2017. Accessed April 25, 2018. http://zenithcity.com/

"The Record of Crime." *Duluth Evening Herald*, March 11, 1893, 1. Minnesota Historical Society, St. Paul, MN. Minnesota Newspaper Digital Hub. Accessed Dec. 7, 2019. https://newspapers.mnhs.org/jsp/browse.jsp.

"The Rounder." *Duluth Evening Herald*, August 7, 1900, 4. Minnesota Historical Society, St. Paul, MN. Minnesota Newspaper Digital Hub. Accessed Dec. 29, 2020. https://newspapers.mnhs.org/jsp/browse.jsp.

"'Tis Lena Olson." *St. Paul Daily Globe*, September 8, 1894, 3. Minnesota Historical Society, St. Paul, MN. Minnesota Newspaper Digital Hub. Accessed Jan. 10, 2021. https://newspapers.mnhs.org/jsp/browse.jsp.

Toponymics and Carto-Etymology. University at Buffalo, New York. Accessed Dec. 18, 2020. http://www.acsu.buffalo.edu/~dbertuca/maps/toponymics.html.

Trenerry, Walter N. *Murder in Minnesota: A Collection of True Cases.* St. Paul: Minnesota Historical Society, 1962.

"Trio of Fiends." *St. Paul Daily Globe*, December 9, 1894, 6. Minnesota Historical Society, St. Paul, MN. Minnesota Newspaper Digital Hub. Accessed Feb. 8, 2021. https://newspapers.mnhs.org/jsp/browse.jsp.

"Truelsen. Opening Meeting of His Campaign Held at the West End." *Duluth Evening Herald*, January 22, 1896, 5. Minnesota Historical Society, St. Paul, MN. Minnesota Newspaper Digital Hub. Accessed Feb. 17, 2021. https://newspapers.mnhs.org/jsp/browse.jsp.

"Two Draymen Wanted." *St. Paul Daily Globe*, September 21, 1894, 3. Minnesota Historical Society, St. Paul, MN. Minnesota Newspaper Digital Hub. Accessed Jan. 13, 2021. https://newspapers.mnhs.org/jsp/browse.jsp.

"Unusual Case of Mistaken Identity." *Duluth News Tribune,* August 25, 1901, 5. Accessed Dec. 16, 2020. https://www.newsbank.com/.

Wade, Stuart C. *Lured to Death or, the Minneapolis Murder: Being an Authentic Account of the Trial, Sentence, Confession and Execution of Harry T. Hayward for the Murder of Miss Catherine M. Ging, with Portraits of the Principals, etc.,* Chicago: E.A. Weeks, 1895.

Watson, Jim. "Wenona Beach Images." Michigan Family History Network. Accessed April 23, 2021. Quote attributed to email dated February 23, 2010. http://www.mifamilyhistory.org/bay/Wenona_Beach.aspx.

Welter, Ben. *Minnesota Mayhem: A History of Calamitous Events, Horrific Accidents, Dastardly Crime and Dreadful Behavior in the Land of Ten Thousand Lakes.* Charleston: History Press, 2012.

"Who Did the Deed?" *The Seattle Post-Intelligencer,* September 7, 1893, 8. Accessed March 1, 2021. https://chroniclingamerica.loc.gov/.

"Who Is Cummings?" *Duluth News Tribune*, August 25, 1894, 1. Accessed Nov. 1, 2013. https://www.newsbank.com/.

"Wilcox Talks of the Verdict." *The Seattle Post-Intelligencer,* February 12, 1894, 8. Accessed March 1, 2021. https://chroniclingamerica.loc.gov/.

"Wild Goose Chase." Source unknown, annotated "February 26, 1896." Northeast Minnesota Historical Center, University of Minnesota-Duluth. Collection: Duluth (City) Police Department Records.

"Will Hold No Inquest." *Duluth Evening Herald*, September 15, 1894, 6. Minnesota Historical Society, St. Paul, MN. Minnesota Newspaper Digital Hub. Accessed Dec. 10, 2020. https://newspapers.mnhs.org/jsp/browse.jsp.

"Will Keep a Watch." *Duluth Evening Herald*, July 19, 1894, 3. Minnesota Historical Society, St. Paul, MN. Minnesota Newspaper Digital Hub. Accessed Dec. 30, 2020. https://newspapers.mnhs.org/jsp/browse.jsp.

Illustration Credits

Chapter One: A Body Found

"Campers." *Duluth Evening Herald*, July 24, 1894, 6. Minnesota Historical Society, St. Paul, MN. Minnesota Newspaper Digital Hub. Accessed Oct. 13, 2021. https://newspapers.mnhs.org/jsp/browse.jsp.

"Minnesota Point streetcar, Duluth, Minnesota. Ca. 1894." Duluth Public Library, Duluth, MN.

"Munger Terrace apartment building under construction, Duluth, Minnesota." 1892. University of Minnesota Duluth, Kathryn A. Martin Library, Northeast Minnesota Historical Collections. Accessed Oct. 13, 2021. https://collection.mndigital.org/catalog/nemhc:1732.

"Superior Street looking east from Seventh Avenue west, Duluth, Minnesota." Ca. 1895. University of Minnesota Duluth, Kathryn A. Martin Library, Northeast Minnesota Historical Collections, Accessed Oct. 13, 2021. https://collection.mndigital.org/catalog/nemhc:15.

"Tugboat *Pathfinder* and crew, Duluth, Minnesota." Ca. 1900. University of Minnesota Duluth, Kathryn A. Martin Library, Northeast Minnesota Historical Collections. Accessed Oct. 13, 2021. https://collection.mndigital.org/catalog/nemhc:1554.

(Sidebar) "The Record of Crime." *Duluth Evening Herald*, March 11, 1893, 1. Minnesota Historical Society, St. Paul, MN. Minnesota Newspaper Digital Hub. Accessed Oct. 13, 2021. https://newspapers.mnhs.org/jsp/browse.jsp.

Chapter Two: The Baffling Mystery

"Barnum and Bailey Greatest Show on Earth." *Duluth Evening Herald*, Aug. 18, 1894, 10. Minnesota Historical Society, St. Paul, MN. Minnesota Newspaper Digital Hub. Accessed Oct. 13, 2021. https://newspapers. mnhs.org/jsp/browse.jsp.

"Picnic on Minnesota Point, Duluth, Minnesota." Ca. 1895. University of Minnesota Duluth, Kathryn A. Martin Library, Northeast Minnesota Historical Collections. Accessed Oct. 13, 2021. https://collection.mndigital.org/catalog/nemhc:2045.

"Oatka Pavilion, Minnesota Point, Duluth, Minnesota." Ca. 1892. Duluth Public Library, Duluth, MN.

"An Unknown Victim." August 1894. University of Minnesota Duluth, Kathryn A. Martin Library, Northeast Minnesota Historical Collections/ Duluth City Police Dept. Records.

(Sidebar) "Someone to Blame." *Duluth Evening Herald*, July 18, 1892, 5. Minnesota Historical Society, St. Paul, MN. Minnesota Newspaper Digital Hub. Accessed Oct. 13, 2021. https://newspapers.mnhs.org/jsp/browse.jsp.

(Sidebar) "Duluth patrol wagon." Ca. 1890. Duluth Public Library, Duluth, MN.

Chapter Three: Identified at Last

"1894 $500 Murder Reward Wanted For A.A. Austin." 1894. Worthpoint. com. Accessed Oct. 21, 2021.

"A Dakota Romance. Girl Supposed to have been dead a year comes home a wife." *Stillwater Messenger*, Oct. 5, 1895, 6. Minnesota Historical Society, St. Paul, MN. Minnesota Newspaper Digital Hub. Accessed Oct. 13, 2021. https://www.mnhs.org/newspapers/hub.

Hoover, Evelyn. "Final resting place for Lena Olson, Lakewood Cemetery, Minneapolis." Oct. 18, 2021.

"Lena Olson." 1894. University of Minnesota Duluth, Kathryn A. Martin Library, Northeast Minnesota Historical Collections/Duluth City Police Dept. Records.

(Sidebar) "Marriage License and Certificate, State of Minnesota (Austin and Olson)." Aug. 20, 1894. Ramsey County Public Health, Vital Records (Marriage Records).

Chapter Four: Pursuit of Suspects

(Image of Detective Bob Benson; sidebar of Chief Armstrong) "Among the Finest." Source unknown, ca. April 1895. University of Minnesota Duluth, Kathryn A. Martin Library, Northeast Minnesota Historical Collections/Duluth City Police Department Records.

"Members of the Duluth Police Department, Duluth, Minnesota." Source unknown, ca. 1889. University of Minnesota Duluth, Kathryn A. Martin Library, Northeast Minnesota Historical Collections. Accessed Oct. 29, 2021. https://collection.mndigital.org/catalog/nemhc:6025.

(Images of Harry T. Hayward, Catherine "Kitty" Ging, and Claus A. Blixt) "Trio of Fiends." *St. Paul Daily Globe,* Dec. 9, 1894, 1. Chronicling America. Accessed Oct. 29, 2021. https://chroniclingamerica.loc.gov/.

(Sidebar) "Duluth Police Headquarters." *History of the Police Department.* W.E. Dindorf & W.J. Gibbons, 1921. Duluth Public Library, Duluth, MN.

Chapter Five: Grasping at Straws

"Harry Hayward, the day before the execution." *Willmar Argus,* Willmar, MN, Dec. 19, 1895, 2. Minnesota Historical Society, St. Paul, MN. Minnesota Newspaper Digital Hub. Accessed Oct. 13, 2021. https://www.mnhs.org/newspapers/hub.

"Not the Right Man." *Minneapolis Tribune,* Jan. 22, 1895, 5. Minnesota Historical Society, St. Paul, MN. Minnesota Newspaper Digital Hub. Accessed Oct. 13, 2021. https://www.mnhs.org/newspapers/hub.

(Image of Meigs County Sheriff's Office) "121-year-old Structure Continues to Serve County." *Point Pleasant Register,* Point Pleasant WV, posted Oct. 7, 2017. Accessed Nov. 19, 2021. https://www.mydailyregister.com/.

Ericson, David. 1910. "Portrait of Henry Truelsen, Mayor 1896–1900, Duluth, Minnesota." Duluth Public Library. Accessed Jan. 30, 2022. https://collection.mndigital.org/catalog/p16022coll6:2096.

(Sidebar) "Desperate Bob Benson Assaults the Editor of The Citizen." *Duluth Citizen,* June 6, 1896, 1. Accessed Feb. 4, 2021. https://newspaperarchive.com/.

Chapter Six: The Final Clues

"Commercial Street, Gilbertsville, New York." Ca. 1890. The Gilbertsville Free Library, Gilbertsville, NY.

"Craven!" *Minneapolis Tribune*, April 19, 1896, 5. Minnesota Historical Society, St. Paul, MN. Minnesota Newspaper Digital Hub. Accessed Jan. 8, 2021. mnhs.org/newspapers/hub.

"East Side, WaKeeney, Kansas." 1885. Trego County Historical Society, WaKeeney, KS.

"Minnehaha Falls, Minneapolis, Minnesota." 1897. Hennepin County Library, James K. Hosmer Special Collections Library. Accessed Nov. 19, 2021. https://collection.mndigital.org/catalog/mpls:24.

"West Hotel, Minneapolis, Minnesota." Ca. 1880–1910. Hennepin County Library, James K. Hosmer Special Collections Library. Accessed Nov. 19, 2021. https://collection.mndigital.org/catalog/mpls:22254.

"William Alsop." Ca. 1880. The Gilbertsville Free Library, Gilbertsville, NY.

Chapter Seven: Descent into Ruin

"Exterior view of the Lake Park Hotel." Ca. 1895. University of Washington, Seattle (UW), Libraries, Special Collections Division, Henry M. Sarvant Photograph Collection, PH Coll. 35, Item #SAR037. Accessed Nov. 20. 2021. http://pcad.lib.washington.edu/building/23464/.

"Horse buggy and woman." Ca. 1890. Author's personal image collection.

Jacoby, William H. "Jacoby's Artistic Minnesota Views; Upton's views of Minnesota and the Northwest; Nicollet Avenue; Jacoby's Minnesota and Northwestern views." Ca. 1880-1890. Hennepin County Library, James K. Hosmer Special Collections Library. Accessed Nov. 19, 2021. https://collection.mndigital.org/catalog/mpls:17.

"Tacoma, Washington." 1890. Author's personal image collection.

Chapter Eight: The Murder Avenged

"Butterworth & Sons, Undertakers." *Seattle and the Orient, Souvenir Edition, Seattle Daily Times,* 1900, 151. Accessed Nov. 11, 2021. Public domain image available via https://commons.wikimedia.org/wiki/Main_Page.

"Seattle city hall and police headquarters." Ca. 1896. University of Washington, Seattle (UW), Libraries, Special Collections Division. Accessed Nov. 11, 2021. Public domain image available via https://commons.wikimedia.org/wiki/Main_Page.

Chapter Nine: Unearthing the Past

"Blanck is No More." *The Seattle Post-Intelligencer*, March 22, 1895, 1. Chronicling America. Accessed Nov. 11, 2021. chroniclingamerica.loc. gov.

"Fortune-Teller." Ca. 1900. Author's personal image collection.

(Sidebar) Brion, Gustave. "Grave Digging." In Victor Hugo's *Les misérables* (Paris: J. Hetzel et A. Lacroix, 1867). Image in Public Domain, courtesy of Univ. of Toronto Libraries, Toronto, Canada. Old Book Illustrations. Accessed Nov. 20, 2021. oldbookillustrations.com.

Epilogue

"Benson's Detective Agency." *Duluth Evening Herald*, March 26, 1896, 8. Minnesota Historical Society, St. Paul, MN. Minnesota Newspaper Digital Hub. Accessed Oct. 13, 2021. https://chttps://www.mnhs.org/newspapers/hub.

"I found this business card ..." Ca. 1908. Posted Oct. 16, 2018, by u/dontgofrank, Reddit.com. Accessed Nov. 22, 2021. https://www.reddit.com/.

"I Remember Way Back When." Ca. 1926. *Minneapolis Daily Star*, March 4, 1926, 7. Newspapers.com. Accessed Aug. 15, 2020. https://www.newspapers.com/.

Notes

Chapter One: A Body Found

[1] The first two paragraphs are a stylized interpretation by the author drawn from "Is All a Mystery," *Duluth News Tribune*, August 23, 1894, 1. Accessed Nov. 7, 2012, Newsbank.com.

Newspaper accounts stated that Guy Browning was nine years old. However, records indicate he was born in 1887 (the 1900 Minnesota census denotes him as thirteen; the 1905 Wisconsin census as eighteen). An assumption was made that Browning was most likely seven when he discovered the body on the beach. (Familysearch.org.)

[2] Quoted in "The Rounder," *Duluth Evening Herald*, August 7, 1900, 4. Accessed Dec. 29, 2020, mnhs.org/newspapers/hub. The following two clippings corroborate Capt. Inman named O-at-ka Beach: "Caught on the Run," *Duluth News Tribune*, June 10, 1901, 4. Accessed Dec. 29, 2020, Newsbank.com; and "Green Room Gossip," *Duluth Evening Herald*, December 27, 1910, 5. Accessed Dec. 29, 2020, mnhs.org/newspapers/hub. To learn more about Inman: collections.mnhs.org/mnhistorymagazine.

The meaning of "O-at-ka" (or Oa-at-ka) is attributed to an Ojibwe word meaning "an opening," presumably named for a clearing of woods found on the sandbar. (Quoted in "The Parks of Minnesota Point," *Zenith City Online*. Accessed April 25, 2018, Zenithcity.com.) In a December 18, 2020, email reply to Jeffrey Sauve as to the origins of the word "O-at-ka," John Nichols, co-author of *A Concise Dictionary of Minnesota Ojibwe* (Minneapolis: University of Minnesota Press, 1995), wrote, "Doesn't look Ojibwe. Given your first spelling [o-at-ka or oa-at-ka], it looks like it might have been named after the boys' camp of that name in Maine." As typical of the era, appropriation of Indigenous people's language was commonplace. Nichols's reference to Camp O-at-ka in Sebago, Maine, is incorrect, as it was founded in 1906, many years removed from naming of the beach on Minnesota Point.

In respect to the Seneca Indian language, the word oa-at-ka means "leaving the highlands or approaching an opening," which is an appropriate moniker, as the city of Duluth was built on a hill. (Toponymics and Carto-Etymology, University at Buffalo, New York. Accessed Dec. 18, 2020, acsu.buffalo.edu.) Other place names using the term "oatka" include: Oatka Creek, Wyoming County, New York; Oatka Cemetery, Wheatland, New York; and Oatka Beach, Traverse City, Michigan. In regard to the latter site, local historian Jim Watson stated, "I believe that 'Oa-at-ka' was a local (Bay City) spelling of oatka or o-at-ka spelled this way and is a Seneca Indian word meaning 'Queen of water.'" (mifamilyhistory.org, accessed April 23, 2021.)

Chapter Two: The Baffling Mystery

[3] Quoted in "Craven!" *Minneapolis Sunday Tribune*, April 19, 1896, 5. Accessed Dec. 14, 2020, mnhs.org/newspapers/hub.

Presumably the two unidentified men were either
Hendrickson, Mike Daugherty, or Edwards (see reference
to "I remember the woman perfectly" and "Several Clews
[sic]").

[4] "She Is Still Dead," *Duluth Sunday News Tribune*, August
26, 1894, 1. Accessed Nov. 1, 2013, Newsbank.com. In the
blurb, Superior, Wisconsin, detective Earnshaw responded
to a question whether he had any opinion as to unraveling
the mysterious murder. "Yes, I have formed an opinion and
I have a clue, supported by a good deal of evidence, but of
course I can't give it to the public before the whole affair
has been investigated and the guilty party is under arrest."
Interestingly, his name never appears in print again in relation to the case.

Chapter Three: Identified at Last

[5] One of the sixteen Lena Olsons living in Minneapolis was
noted in "Just Like a Woman," *Minneapolis Tribune*, October
13, 1894, 5. Accessed Jan. 8, 2021, mnhs.org/newspapers/
hub. The brief clipping read: "Albert Hagen, thirty-three
years of age, was arrested last night on a warrant sworn out
by a servant girl named Lena Olson, charging him with being the father of her unborn child. Lena called to see Hagen
early in the evening and remained by his cell a greater part
of the evening. She wanted the jailer to let him out, claiming
to feel sorry for having had him locked up."

[6] From the very beginning of the murder case, the engraved
bangles worn by Lena Olson were noted to have included
"Mabel" and "May." When Lizzie Olson positively identified
the bracelet, she was recorded as saying "Mabel" stood for a

brother Erick's wife, and "May," a brother's child. However, South Dakota census records indicate that Erick P. Olson's wife was named Mary, and they had a daughter named Mabel. In addition, Øyane's *Gards og Ættesoga for Luster Kommune* also confirms that Erick was married to a woman named Mary. (Familysearch.org, accessed Dec. 30, 2020; and "Positively Identified," *Duluth Evening Herald*, September 10, 1894, 2. Accessed Jan. 12, 2021, mnhs.org/newspapers/hub.)

[7] On the same day, Sunday, September 9, 1894, another body washed up on the rocks near Lester Park; Duluth's third floater in the past three weeks. The man, whose approximate age was fifty-five, was lying partly in the water, face downward, with the upper portion resting on the rocks. His bloated and badly decomposed corpse was naked except for a torn and bloodied light undershirt. The police and attending physicians immediately announced that he had taken his own life. However, others in the community believed he was murdered. Within days, the man was identified as Christ Frederickson, a Swedish book peddler employed by a Chicago firm. Described as a genial, happy fellow, Frederickson was known to sometimes carry large sums of money on his person before remitting funds to the publisher. In the end, Coroner Eklund decided not to hold an inquest and maintained death came by suicide. ("Another Body Found," *Duluth Evening Herald*, September 10, 1894, 2; and "Will Hold No Inquest," *Duluth Evening Herald*, September 15, 1894, 6. Accessed Dec. 10, 2020, mnhs.org/newspapers/hub.)

[8] According to the Lakewood Cemetery burial records, Lena Olson's final interment was section PG11, Row 12, Grave 8

(public/single grave). Place of death given as "Duluth." Her date of death was listed as September 12, 1894. In actuality, that is the date of burial, as she was murdered on August 21. (Lakewood Cemetery Funeral and Grave Search, Lakewood Cemetery, Minneapolis, MN. Accessed March 19, 2021, lakewoodcemetery.org/burial-search.)

[9] Quoted in "Lena Olson's Money," *Minneapolis Tribune*, September 16, 1894, 7. Accessed Jan. 8, 2021, mnhs.org/newspapers/hub. Clay also stated that Austin represented himself as "the agent of Eastern capitalists, who were the alleged owners of lands, which Austin claimed it was his business in Minneapolis to sell if possible."

[10] From the onset of the Lena Olson murder case, authorities stated that the motive was straightforward: she was killed for her money. Mrs. Clay reported Olson had entrusted her with $450 and then asked for $47 of it for railroad fare needed to visit her brother Erick in Edgerton, South Dakota. Clay then gave her $50. Olson never gave Clay any intimation that she had entered into a relationship with Austin. Upon saying their farewells, Olson told her employer that she would make arrangements for the disposition of the rest of her money, which she planned to use to help her brother complete his homestead. ("Lena Olson's Money," *Minneapolis Tribune*, September 16, 1894, 7. Accessed Dec. 1, 2021, mnhs.org/newspapers/hub.) The bigger question without an answer is how much money did Olson actually have on her person when departing for Duluth? Austin most likely would not have killed her for the paltry train fare alone. More than likely, Olson had more than several hundred dollars on her. After having committed murder, Austin

returned to the Twin Cities and visited Olson's friend, Emma Olson. He did not call on Clay, presumably because he was unaware of the savings she held for Lena Olson.

[11] Quoted in "Proofs Are Furnished," *Duluth Evening Herald*, September 13, 1897, 5. Accessed Feb. 7, 2019, mnhs.org/newspapers/hub. For narrative clarity, Rev. Barker's quotes were rearranged. See sidebar "Nuptials Naught?"

Chapter Four: Pursuit of Suspects

[12] Quoted in "Desperate Bob Benson Assaults the Editor of The Citizen," *Duluth Citizen*, June 6, 1896, 1. Accessed Feb. 4, 2021, Newspaperarchive.com. The 1880 Michigan census noted Robert Benson, seventeen, lived in Montcalm County and worked in a mill.

[13] Quoted in "Arthur Austin. Was Arrested in New Orleans. Charged with Lena Olson's Murder," *Duluth News Tribune*, December 15, 1894, 1. Accessed Nov. 7, 2012, Newsbank. com. For grammatical clarity, the sentence was rephrased from the printed version: " 'My God! Arthur's arrested for murder,' fainted."

Chapter Five: Grasping at Straws

[14] Quoted in "Know His Face," *Duluth News Tribune*, January 20, 1895, 1. Accessed Nov. 9, 2012, Newsbank.com. Some newspapers incorrectly cited that Thea Larson, a friend of Lena Olson's, accompanied Detective Benson to Chicago. In addition, the exact same image of Joseph Adams, alias James Driscoll, was also featured in the *Minneapolis Tribune* on March 9, 1895, as that of Claus A. Blixt, the "man who shot and killed Miss Ging."

[15] Ibid. Emphasis added.

[16] Ibid. Emphasis and restatement added to the original quote, "That is Austin."

[17] Quoted in "Cleverly Trapped," *Minneapolis Tribune*, January 21, 1895, 5. Accessed Nov. 21, 2012, Newsbank.com. Emphasis added to quote.

[18] Quoted in "Another Austin Found. An Ohio Sheriff Thinks He Has the Murderer," *Duluth Evening Herald*, February 15, 1896, 6. Accessed Nov. 21, 2012, Newsbank. com. In the original clipping, the name of the sheriff was signed "H.E. Ashbury." The correct name of the sheriff from Meigs County, OH, was Aurin P. Ashworth (b. 1857).

[19] Quoted in "Is Surely the Man," *Duluth News Tribune*, February 20, 1896, 4. Accessed Nov. 7, 2012, Newsbank. com. "Sheriff Ashbury" changed to "Sheriff Ashworth" for accuracy.

[20] "It Is Not Austin," *Duluth News Tribune*, February 22, 1896, 5. Accessed Nov. 15, 2012, Newsbank.com. In August 1901, Detective Benson was interviewed by the Duluth News Tribune regarding his experiences working on the Lena Olson murder case. In regard to the Pomeroy, OH, episode, Benson recalled: "Another time I was called down to Ohio on the same case and was met by the sheriff who told me all about the arrest and that there was no possible chance for a mistake. When the suspect was shown me I nearly threw a fit. Austin was about thirty-seven years old and quite heavy, while the man before me was ten years younger and forty pounds lighter. The sheriff insisted that he was the murderer

all right, notwithstanding the differences I showed him, and protested vigorously because I couldn't see it that way. While he was absent from the room a minute the prisoner whispered that he hoped I would identify him as Austin because he wanted to get out to Duluth but was a little short on railroad fare. I told him that I didn't think the state of Minnesota was quite ready to put up for him." ("Unusual Case of Mistaken Identity," *Duluth News Tribune*, August 25, 1901, 5. Accessed Dec. 16, 2020, Newsbank.com.)

Chapter Six: The Final Clues

[21] Quoted in "Dead!," *Minneapolis Tribune*, April 18, 1896, 1. Accessed Feb. 22, 2021, mnhs.org/newspapers/hub. The name Albert, which is later learned, was inserted in the quote for clarity. Mrs. Guimond (also known as Mrs. Patwell) was also quoted in the press that Ellenson first arrived at her house on Thanksgiving Day, 1893. Other references state he boarded during the summer months of 1894. For the sake of continuity, which is later supported by additional evidence, he arrived March 21, 1894, (a few days before Easter) and remained until April 26.

[22] Family pedigree charts on Ancestry.com and Familysearch. org place James E. Alsop's birth at either Marylebone, Middlesex (site of his parents' marriage in 1840), or Rickmansworth, Hertfordshire. However, there was a "James Allsop" born in the second quarter of 1846, Ashbourne, Derbyshire (name of parents not provided). Author unable to determine full middle name.

[23] John, the eldest child, suffered a horrific accident on August 5, 1880. *The Morris Chronicle* recounted:

"Butternuts.—Last Thursday afternoon John Alsop, son of James Alsop, of Gilbertsville, aged about thirteen years, was out hunting. In getting over a fence his gun, which was at half-cock, was accidentally discharged, contents entering the young lad's breast, tearing the flesh in a fearful manner, and then glanced off his breast bone into the under jaw, breaking the latter in two places. He was discovered soon after by persons building [a] fence, who heard the report of his gun and heard his groans, and [was] taken home. Five pieces of bone were taken from the wounds, before they were dressed. At this writing, (Saturday), he lies in a critical condition." ("Vicinity and County News," *The Morris Chronicle*, Morris, NY, August 11, 1880, 3. Accessed Dec. 1, 2021, morris. advantage-preservation.com.) Although John recovered from his ordeal, he later succumbed to smallpox and died in Tacoma, WA Territory, January 1889.

[24] Charles "Henry" Alsop married Phoebe J. Lambert in 1886, Rooks County, KS. They had three sons. She died in 1908; he passed away at the age of seventy-seven at San Diego, CA. There is a possibility that in his early Kansas years he suffered a tragic farm accident. A "Henry Alsop" was noted in a September 1884 issue of the Allen County newspaper that his hand was caught in the gearing of a thresher, and "crushed so badly that it had to be amputated across the palm."

After an extensive summer tour of Kansas, Adelbert "Delbert" Alsop returned in September 1881 to Gilbertsville. After a brief time, he ventured back to Kansas where, in 1884, he married Anna Enstrom. They settled in Trego County and had eight children. In 1896, he was assaulted with a four-tined pitchfork wielded by Philetus H. Smith. The defendant appealed his case to the Kansas State Supreme Court. The guilty verdict was affirmed. The court stated Smith was convicted of wounding Alsop under such circumstances as would have constituted manslaughter in the fourth degree if death had ensued. Several years later, Alsop and family moved to Lafayette, Oregon. He died of unspecified "internal injuries" on February 6, 1907, age forty-nine.

[25] Quoted in "Boys on a Bum," *Western Kansas World*, WaKeeney, KS, May 28, 1887, 5. Accessed Feb. 23, 2021, Chroniclingamerica.loc.gov. For his brief stint as marshal, Alsop was noted several times in the local newspaper, such as this story: "Last Friday night, Geo. Brooks brought a couple of drunken men whom he found riding around the prairie. They were both lying in the bottom of the wagon, and there [sic] team had no driver. They were turned over to City Marshall [sic] Alsop, who packed them comfortably up in the wagon and left the team in charge of one of the livery stables. Next morning they were taken before Police Judge Hutzel, and fined $1.00 each and costs." (*Western Kansas World*, March 5, 1887, 4. Accessed Feb. 23, 2021, Chroniclingamerica.loc.gov.)

Chapter Seven: Descent into Ruin

[26] Quoted in *Jean Sensel*, Spanaway, West Columbia, SC: Arcadia Publishing, 2014, 42. Accessed March 1, 2021, google.com/books. The unincorporated community of Spanaway, WA, boasted a population of 35,000 in 2020.

[27] Quoted in "Dashed to Death," source unknown, ca.
November 1890. Clipping found in local history collection scrapbook #S-5-69 kept by Florence Stebbins, The
Gilbertsville Free Library, Gilbertsville, NY. Alsop added
that "she died in a few minutes," but other accounts state
she lingered for a few hours. When daughter Kate, twelve,
heard of her mother's death, she exclaimed, "My mamma
is in Heaven." Her remark "brought tears to the eyes of all
who heard her." ("A Terrible Death," *Western Kansas World*,
WaKeeney, KS, December 6, 1890, 4. Accessed Feb. 23,
2021, Chroniclingamerica.loc.gov.)

[28] Quoted in "A Villain," *Duluth Evening Herald*, April 27,
1896, 2. Accessed March 1, 2020, mnhs.org/newspapers/
hub. The informant's name was not provided but was described as a "well known resident of Tacoma."

[29] The case against William A. Wilcox for the murder of
Charlotte Fetting was a drawn-out affair. After he was tried
three times, he was finally convicted of manslaughter and
sentenced to twenty years. As for his explanation as to why
he had chloroform in his possession (a drug used to subdue
Fetting), he told *The Seattle Post-Intelligencer*: "I had suffered
for nearly three months, and someone in the barber shop
recommended chloroform and bay rum. ... when it came
to buying the drug I would have done so myself only that I
owed Studress [drug store] about $15." ("Wilcox Talks of
the Verdict," *The Seattle Post-Intelligencer*, February 12, 1894,
8. Accessed March 1, 2021, Chroniclingamerica.loc.gov.)
The barber also testified that Wilcox purchased some rum
and chloroform from him to cure a "private disease." Wilcox

appealed his conviction and secured his acquittal in February 1895.

Chapter Eight: The Murder Avenged

[30] Quoted in "Reads Like Holmes," *The Seattle Post-Intelligencer*, April 17, 1896, 8. Accessed March 2, 2021, Chroniclingamerica.loc.gov. The name Alsop was corrected from "Allsop." Detective Courtney also gave an interview to the *Minneapolis Tribune*. ("A Fiend!," *Minneapolis Tribune*, April 26, 1896, 1. Accessed March 3, 2021, mnhs.org/newspapers/hub.) The interviews he provided to both newspapers differ slightly, and are synthesized and reorganized for a more accurate narrative regarding the capture of James E. Alsop.

[31] Ibid. In the account published by *The Seattle Post-Intelligencer*, Courtney commenced his vigil at six a.m., and Alsop first appeared to pick up his mail at three p.m.

[32] Quoted in "Strangled to Death," *The Seattle Post-Intelligencer*, April 18, 1896, 8. Accessed March 2, 2021, Chroniclingamerica.loc.gov. The name Alsop was corrected from "Allsop."

[33] From quotes "His nerve is breaking" to "I feel very sorry about his committing suicide" are synthesized from two sources, "Strangled to Death" and "Reads like Holmes." The sentence, "Where in the devil is Alsop?' he muttered to Courtney," was created for narrative purposes. The quote "Cut him down!" originally was printed as "Cut it down."

[34] The nefarious iron bolt from which James E. Alsop hanged

himself on April 17, 1896, again tempted the life of another several years later. On May 4, 1900, a New York native named C.N. Barron, twenty-three, unsuccessfully attempted to "batter his brains against the iron hook." The attempted suicide was briefly detailed in *The Seattle Post-Intelligencer*:

> *Against the same iron hook in the women's ward of the city jail from which James E. Allsop [sic], a notorious criminal, hanged himself rather than return to Duluth to stand trial for a brutal murder, C.N. Barron, of New York, yesterday afternoon attempted to batter out his own brains. He dashed his head against the hook, cutting deep gashes in his scalp, and covering the walls and floor of his cell with blood. A woman confined in another cell heard the noise made by Barron when he threw himself against the wall. She raised the alarm. Jailer Corning rushed in and caught Barron just as he was making a lunge. Dripping with blood, the prisoner was taken out into the big cell and inspected. He was a pitiful sight to behold. The following day he was "committed to the insane asylum by Judge Moore upon the certificate of two physicians that his mind was unbalanced."*

("Attempts Suicide in Jail," *The Seattle Post-Intelligencer*, May 5, 1900, 5; and "Barron is Insane," *The Seattle Post-Intelligencer*, May 6, 1900, 18. Accessed March 1, 2021, Chroniclingamerica.loc.gov.)

[35] Quoted in "Nobody Wants It," *The Seattle Post-Intelligencer*, April 19, 1896, 8. Accessed March 3, 2021, Chroniclingamerica.loc.gov. The name Alsop was corrected from "Allsop."

[36] Quoted in "Craven!," *Minneapolis Tribune*, April 19, 1896, 5. Accessed March 3, 2021, mnhs.org/newspapers/hub. The name

Alsop was corrected from "Allsop." Detective Benson was referring to the April 18, 1896, issue of the *Minneapolis Tribune*.

Epilogue

[37] Quoted in John J. Courtney, "A Woman's Hunch Put Me on Track of Murderer Year After Crime," *Minneapolis Daily Star*, March 4, 1926, 7. Accessed Aug. 15, 2020, Newspapers. com. As for the $250 reward from the State of Minnesota, the payment was issued to Detective Courtney on August 21, 1896, exactly two years to the day Lena Olson was killed.

In the matter of the $250 payment from the St. Louis County commissioners, Courtney narrowly received it due to the fact that Alsop was not tried and convicted per the original terms of the reward. Immediately following Alsop's suicide, photographs of the murderer were taken and disseminated. Not all those familiar with Alsop agreed the images resembled him. After returning to Minnesota, Courtney visited with Lizzie Olson, who had returned to Minneapolis, and two of Lena's intimate friends, Thea Larson and Mrs. Julia Burreson. The women were shown pictures of Alsop, which each immediately identified as A.A. Austin. Courtney then procured from them affidavits and headed up to Duluth to claim his reward. The county commissioners voted 3–2 in favor of paying the detective. ("Proceedings of the Board of County Commissioners of St. Louis County, Minnesota," *Duluth Evening Herald*, August 1, 1896, 10. Accessed Nov. 21, 2012, Newsbank.com.)

[38] To learn more about the shocking crime, see Heidi Bakk-Hansen's story, "The Slaying of Dr. J.J. Eklund," at zenithcity. com.

About the Author

Jeffrey M. Sauve has been featured in the Minneapolis *StarTribune*, Minnesota Historical Society's MNopedia, MinnPost, MPR Radio, and TPT television. An award-winning author and historian, Sauve has written eight books and scores of articles for local and regional publications. After

serving 20 years as an archivist at St. Olaf College in Northfield, Minnesota, he pursued a successful writing career. Titles by Sauve include: *Pioneer Women: Voices of Northfield's Frontier* (2009); *Dear Santa, Mama Wants Hat Pins, Papa, One Mule: A Compilation of Letters from the Northfield News, 1902–1945* (2012); *Milestones and Memories of the St. Olaf Band, 1891–2018* (2019), of which he was co-author; and *St. Olaf Theater: A Centennial Celebration, 1921–2021* (2021).

Jeffrey M. Sauve, author. Courtesy of author.